# ESSAYS AND ADDRESSES

# ESSAYS
# AND ADDRESSES

*by*

OLIVER ELTON

*Essay Index Reprint Series*

 BOOKS FOR LIBRARIES PRESS
FREEPORT, NEW YORK

STANDARD BOOK NUMBER:
8369-1179-2


LIBRARY OF CONGRESS CATALOG CARD NUMBER:
77-86746


PRINTED IN THE UNITED STATES OF AMERICA

# *Preface*

The lectures and essays that are here gathered in are not altogether a miscellany. Three are on English poets; four are on Slavonic writers, whom I have studied in amateur fashion and chiefly of late years. Two, of a more abstract kind, owe much to the old, the never quite forgotten, discipline of 'Greats'. A critic of literature, though he may be well aware that he is no philosopher, may still try as it were to look through the railings, and to ask what philosophy can teach him about his business. It will introduce him to 'poetic', which is the theory of poetry, or rather of artistic invention generally; and I have talked about poetic and its history to more generations of college students than I care to reckon up. The brief notices at the end of the book are inserted *in piam memoriam* of two scholars whom I have been happy to count as friends.

Acknowledgments, and thanks for permission to reprint, are offered: to the British Academy, for *Style in Shakespeare*; to the *Review of English Studies*, for *Byron*; to the English Association and Oxford University Press, for *Robert Bridges and*

5

## Preface

'*The Testament of Beauty*'; to the same Press, and to the Taylorian Institution, for *Chekhov*; to the Manchester University Press, for *Literary Criticism*, and also (with the English Association and Oxford Press) for *Reason and Enthusiasm*; to Mr. Archer M. Huntington and the Hispanic Society of America, for *James Fitzmaurice-Kelly*; to *Life and Letters Today*, for *George Saintsbury*, and also for the free use of an article, here much expanded, on *Karel Čapek*.

For this last, I am indebted for valued advice to Dr. René Wellek, of the London School of Slavonic Studies. Also, for the use of their translations in *Pushkin*, to the Hon. Maurice Baring, Sir Bernard Pares, and Professor R. M. Hewitt. This lecture is reprinted by leave of the Royal Institution of Great Britain.

Some further obligations are mentioned in the Notes. Many of the articles have been slightly revised.

O. E.

Oxford,
*May* 1939.

6

# Contents

7

# Style in Shakespeare

## I

Any one who tries to speak at large upon this subject must feel soon dashed, and a little o'er-parted, like Sir Nathaniel in *Love's Labour's Lost*. Shakespeare has not one style, but many. We might think them the work of several different authors—if we did not know better. There is his own, in his narrative poems and sonnets; and there are all the voices, the individual voices, of the great invented population. What is there left, or rather what is there not left, to say about them? Can we, with any profit, begin to classify these styles, according to the speakers that use them, the occasions that beget them, the stagecraft that requires them? Have they any definite history visible, as the dramatist's power expands? Science and scholarship, of course, have begun to furnish answers to such questions. I will not try to recount here the benefactors [n]—lexicographers, grammarians, metrists, editors, biographers—to whom we are in debt; and am not pretending to add one stone to that pyramid of lore; in this Academy, it is enough to salute it in passing. The normal playgoer, the unprofessional

9

reader, is hardly aware of its magnitude; or he
might simply be daunted; he might begin to doubt
the truth of a saying of Miss Ellen Terry, which is
rather in the vein of her delightful Beatrice, by some
few of us still so well remembered: 'Coroners' in-
quests cannot make Shakespeare into a dead man.'
That is true—if not quite as the speaker meant it.
These learned operations do not kill Shakespeare;
no, they quicken him for us beyond measure. We
can begin, in the schoolboy's sense, to construe him,
that is, to know better what his words meant to
his first hearers; to realize the vast store of them, it
is said some 20,000, which he uses; and how he
dragged out many a word, phrase, or usage from
literary or common speech, sometimes from the
grosser underworld of language, and has passed
many a one into our common parlance; how even
his commonest terms often have a shade of meaning
which now is lost, and which, not without stiff
application, we must try to grasp. Everything has
been analysed for our benefit; his grammar, his
compounds, his proverbs, his use of slang and
dialects, and his oaths. The metrists have been
no less active; their labours have been prodigious.
His versification [n] has been studied statistically;
although, in the nature of the case, the findings,
where so much depends on the ear, cannot always
agree. His rhymed, his lengthened, his shortened
lines have been tabled in terms of percentages;
also the lines that are 'split' between two speakers,
and those which end on so weak an accent that the

voice is more or less forbidden to pause. It is all indispensable evidence. The actuarial study of metre, and to some extent of language, is, to begin with, a supplement in aid of that bedrock problem, the approximate, the partly conjectured, order of the plays.

Still, all this science (and of textual science I am saying nothing) has been less often used to illuminate Shakespeare's artistic mastery of language and rhythm; and I can only offer stray notes on that immense question. My illustrations will be taken largely from plays written before 1600. Let us think of his style, not in its constituent atoms, the word or the foot, but regarded rather as the product of the characters, the passions, the situations, which in fact are the living, the driving forces behind and *determining* the style.

II

The critics of a century ago (they are still our greatest critics) had next to no science, and yet they went deep. Coleridge and Hazlitt were chiefly bent on praising the poet's inspiration and his judgement and with reading, or reading into, his dramatis personæ; they also had inspired flashes when they spoke of his verbal and dramatic craft. What can be better than De Quincey's account of his method in dialogue? It touches on the living nerve that links the changing emotion of the speakers with the figures of speech that lie dead before us in the grammars. I shall follow it with a familiar example.

Every form of natural interruption, breaking through the restraints of ceremony under the impulses of tempestuous passion; every form of hasty interrogative, ardent reiteration when a question has been evaded; every form of hostile repetition of the hostile words; every impatient continuation of the hostile statement; in short, all modes and formulæ by which anger, hurry, fretfulness, scorn, impatience, or excitement under any movement whatever, can disturb or modify the formal bookish style of commencement—these are as rife in Shakespeare's dialogue as in life itself.

*Cas.* I said, an elder soldier, not a better:
  Did I say 'better'?
*Bru.*     If you did, I care not.
*Cas.* When Cæsar lived, he durst not thus have moved me.
*Bru.* Peace, peace! you durst not so have tempted him.
*Cas.* I durst not!
*Bru.*     No.
*Cas.* What! durst not tempt him!
*Bru.*       For your life you durst not.
*Cas.* Do not presume too much upon my love;
  I may do that I shall be sorry for.

Later interpreters, who were also scholars, such as the honoured Edward Dowden and Andrew Bradley,[n] spoke with much nicety on Shakespeare's form; but they too were more concerned with penetrating his characters, or his philosophy of life. To-day the gap between hard learning and artistic comment continues to be filled. Fresh in mind is the service of Miss Caroline Spurgeon, with her ordered account of *Shakespeare's Imagery*[n]; and nearer still to the scene in which he moved and had his being are the *Prefaces* of Mr. Granville-Barker, which illuminate the value of the poet's words, and sounds, and silences, as heard in the theatre, and the indivisible tie between the imaginary speaker's nature and his utterance.

What, then, is the right line of approach to the study of the poet's style, of his many styles? The siege, plainly, must be made from two sides. We must, with all the aids of science, work upward from the word, and from the unit of rhythm; but also downward, starting from the conception, the character, and the situation. Words and measures are after all only the artist's material; what is it that *directs* his choice and use of them? We may assume that in the inventive process of drama the words, at any rate, do not come first. Sometimes they may do so, and may tempt the poet to place them with only a show of plausibility; it may be so when he bestows the sublime lines on the heavenly orbs and their patines of bright gold upon a rather ordinary young eloping Venetian who is sitting out under their light. But as a rule the story comes first; the story that Shakespeare, as we know, took from where he would and shaped as he would; and then come the situations; people acting, suffering, moving and pausing, clashing and interacting. 'Persons influence us,' says Cardinal Newman, 'voices melt us . . . deeds inflame us'; and so it is in the mental theatre of the dramatist. *They* decide the language and shape the harmonies. It is

13

for us to start, if we can, with his men and women, and with their plight of embroiling circumstance, and then to listen for their voices; so following, however afar off, the order of invention. If this seem self-evident, let it pass for a line of approach that is not always followed.

One other submission I shall make in passing, though it does not admit of direct proof; namely, that Shakespeare was a far more conscious and deliberate craftsman in words and sounds than is sometimes admitted. However fast he may have written, nay often must have written; however rare or disputed may be the evidence for his revision of his text; however little he may have cared to blot, and however much he may have suffered for it; yet, a hundred times over, we cannot think of his perfection in style as just instinctive or spontaneous. It can have all the effect of calculated art. He did not use our pedantic terms; but when he wrote 'the multitudinous seas incarnadine', or the Clown's picture in *Twelfth Night* of Malvolio's prison, that it 'hath bay windows transparent as barricadoes, and the clearstores toward the south north are as lustrous as ebony'—did he not study every syllable like a connoisseur? But I will leave the rest of my quotations to-day to enforce this plea.

III

In fact, we can glean something about Shakespeare's own tastes and dislikes in the matter of

style. In the Sonnets he speaks for himself; but
the words of his personages, too, are often stamped
with his clear approval, and it seems fair to quote
them. We feel this when Portia discourses on the
quality of mercy; where the poet, as so often, is a
deliberate and even obtrusive moralizer; and why
not also when he speaks of language? Indeed,
good style in his eyes approaches to a moral quality,
twice blest. Most of all, he seems to prize simplicity in expression, as in character. The word
'simple', no doubt, often meant foolish or rustically
naïve; but not so when Juliet calls true love acted
simple modesty; and we hear of simple faith, or of
truth's simplicity. For language, the favourite
word is 'plain', in nearly the same sense. Before
Claudio, in *Much Ado*, was in love, he would 'speak
plain and to the purpose, like an honest man and a
soldier'. The Sonnets contrast the poet's 'true
plain words' with the 'gross painting' used by others.
He abjures 'what strainèd touches rhetoric can
lend', also 'new-found methods and compounds
strange'; although, indeed, Shakespeare abounds in
these himself. The song 'Come away, come away,
death', is called 'old and plain', and 'silly-sooth',
or truth unsophisticated. Amiens commends the
Duke's praises of the woodland life in Arden, they
have been expressed in 'so quiet and so sweet a
style'—an obvious motto for the play itself. Rosalind speaks of Phebe's letter as in a 'boisterous and
a cruel style'; and the poet, looking back, may or
may not have thought how often this term had been

applicable to his own *Richard III*. The word
'phrase' is often contemptuous, especially in *Hamlet*.
We hear of a vile phrase, or a grandsire phrase.
In *Troilus and Cressida*, Pandarus says, 'My business
seethes'; to which a Servant replies, 'Sodden business! there's a stewed phrase indeed!'. Justice
Shallow commends 'good phrases', when Bardolph
has observed that 'a soldier is better accommodated
than with a wife'. 'It comes of *accommodo*; very
good; a good phrase.' All this points to a distaste
for artifice in speech, and is akin to Hamlet's advice
on elocution to the players. Yet Shakespeare also
values magnificence; he envies, in the rival poet, the
'proud full sail of his great verse'. It might be a
good description of his own verse when he begins,
as his habit is, an English history play with an
organ-note:

> So shaken as we are, so wan with care,
> Find we a time for frighted peace to pant
> And breathe short-winded accents of new broils
> To be commenced in stronds afar remote.

In the Sonnets, again, style, in the sense of something rich and strange and elaborate, written with a
'golden quill', and in 'precious phrase by all the
Muses filled', is spoken of as something outside
Shakespeare's own range. The beloved youth will
not get that from *him*; but will say, making his
comparisons, 'Theirs for their style I'll read, his for
his love'. And there are yet other references to
beauty of diction. Holofernes is not himself a

simple speaker; but he admires, in a famous phrase, 'the elegancy, facility, and golden cadence of poesy'; and he is thinking of a poet who counts for something in Shakespeare's narratives:

> Ovidius Naso was the man; and why, indeed, Naso, but for smelling out the odoriferous flowers of fancy, the jerks of invention?

Put these two passages together and we begin to have a just criticism of *Venus and Adonis*. A valuable paper by Miss G. D. Willcock on *Shakespeare as Critic of Language* [n] throws light on the changes which, during his youth, came over the speech and literary taste of the time. *Love's Labour's Lost*, in which those changes are described as 'the dominant theme', furnishes Miss Willcock with an excellent text, on which I therefore need not dwell.

## IV

Shakespeare's hints thus tell us something of his preferences, though naturally they do not suggest half the glories, or all the drawbacks, of his style. But there are many other signs of his distaste for artificial speech, and also of his skill in constructing it for the dramatic purpose. False style of many kinds, and betraying many motives, is as abundant in his plays as in real life. It may be the jargon of vanity, like that of the Poet in *Timon of Athens*. The manner may be literary and topical; when Pistol rants about the 'pampered jades of Asia', Marlowe's phrase is still fresh in the memory of the theatre. So, too, with the bombast of the inserted plays in *Hamlet*; and that drama is the great hunting-ground for specimens of unreal style, for five at least of the characters drop into it. Hamlet himself, in his 'antic disposition', or genuine distraction—as in his wrangle with Laertes in Ophelia's grave (that barbarous business)—exactly disobeys his own counsel to the players to observe the modesty of nature: a counsel which we all take as Shakespeare's own. Hamlet is a great verbal critic; he has the sharpest of ears for affectation; he mocks and mimics Osric, a being who *is* nothing more than the words he speaks—and these are nothing. Hamlet plays with his old mates the two courtiers, one-dimensional creatures, who have their own spurious court idiom. But in the public speech of Claudius there is the darker shade of falsity; just as in the professions of Cordelia's sisters, or in the extravagance of Macbeth's imagery, when the murder has come out and he must needs put a face upon it;

> Here lay Duncan,
> His silver skin laced with his golden blood.

But here there is a further refinement; for the memory of his real terror at the sight of his handiwork comes back to Macbeth, and also, for the moment, gives to his histrionics the required thrill of sincerity. If we ever feel that these devices are all too palpable, and that Shakespeare forces the note, we remember that they are in the nature of directions to the actor, and also that he had to make them 'carry' to the farthest ends of the house, and to the simplest spectator.    But in one personage, who might plausibly be called Shakespeare's greatest stylist, such emphasis would have been inartistic. The words of Iago must not bear on their face the stamp of falsity; we are far indeed from Richard Crookback, whose victims seem to us so foolish. In soliloquy Iago can be plain and brutal, nay almost flat; but when he joins in the dialogue, in verse or prose, what a virtuoso of language!    How he enjoys it for its own sake, and rolls it on his tongue!    He is more than blunt or bluff, as befits the honest man; in his allocution to Roderigo he is a natural orator; repeating, and spacing out, his almost lyrical refrain, 'put money in thy purse', like Shylock with 'let him look to his bond'; dwelling on long or unusual words and on their cadence, 'perdurable', 'sequestration', 'supersubtle', 'sanctimony'; and he even turns euphuist, somewhat late in the day, with his balanced clauses and his allusion to a polysyllabic vegetable:

These Moors are changeable in their wills:—fill thy purse with money:—the food that to him now is luscious as locusts, shall be to him shortly as bitter as coloquintida.

I must not speak of the actor's contribution to the effect; but merely to read the colloquy with Othello is to feel how the words 'Honest, my lord!', 'Think, my lord!', and the rest, are economized, dropping in minims from the vial; and how the climax comes in the mock oath, so terribly near to real poetry:

19

Witness, you ever-burning lights above,
You elements that clip us round about,
Witness that here Iago doth give up
The execution of his wit, hands, heart,
To wrong'd Othello's service.

Does the poet here give a hint of artifice, by this somewhat archaic, Marlowe-like use of the third person for the names, in mock solemnity?

All such effects suggest anything but careless ease in composition. As to the poet's precepts of plainness, simplicity, and directness, it is clear that he did not always practise them; I mean, of course, not only that he can be rich and magnificent, with all the glories of his imagery, at any moment and for whole scenes on end, but that he can, notoriously, write in a complex and embarrassed style, which must have been difficult for his own audience, and which sometimes has, and sometimes has not, a dramatic aim and justification. To this feature of his later tragedies I must return; but meantime we can point to certain occasions on which it is Shakespeare's habit, first and last, to revert to simplicity, even to bareness; and this not least in the plays that abound in ravelled language. Simplicity, on its negative side, is but the removal of barriers between mind and mind, between heart and heart; and it is usually present at the important moments of the drama; at the great crises, in the great farewells, and in the great reconciliations. These utterances *have* to be plain, if they are to 'carry' far, and everywhere, and immediately. Macbeth's 'I am settled', Othello's

'All my fond love thus do I blow to heaven', Hamlet's 'The rest is silence'—the examples crowd upon us, like Imogen's 'Why did you throw your wedded lady from you?'

V

One other trait has often been dwelt upon: that women's speech in Shakespeare, as in life, is as a rule straighter, plainer, less figured and literary, than the speech of men. De Quincey,[n] in his essay on *Style*, remarks that 'the educated women of Great Britain . . . are the true and best depositaries of the old mother idiom'; and further, in words that bring us back to Hermione and Desdemona, that

> No woman in this world, under a movement of resentment from a false accusation, or from jealousy, or from confidence betrayed, ever was at leisure to practise vagaries of caprice in the management of her mother tongue: strength of real feeling shuts out all temptation to the affectation of false feeling.

The words apply best to tragedy or tragi-comedy; we think of Imogen's

> False to his bed! what is it to be false?
> To lie in watch there and to think on him?
> To weep 'twixt clock and clock?

But in comedy the speech of Shakespeare's ladies need not be so simple. Beatrice, an enjoyer of language, abounds in figure and verbal subtlety;

her prose has a distinct, almost a scannable, cadence of its own, which is unlike that of Rosalind; while that of Portia, talking with Nerissa, is patterned, with its balance and hunting of the letter, upon the still familiar style of euphuism.[n]

> The brain may devise laws for the blood, but a hot temper leaps o'er a cold decree: such a hare is madness the youth, to skip o'er the meshes of good counsel the cripple . . . so is the will of a living daughter curbed by the will of a dead father.

Students have shown how Shakespeare, that gay borrower, almost to the last liked to echo John Lyly's tune or to inlay his phrases; and how, throughout, his prose profited by the discipline. Long afterwards, unexpectedly, we come on Goldsmith praising Lyly's writing as 'a kind of prodigy of neatness, clearness, and precision'.

The complex Helena in *All's Well*, the only thinker amongst Shakespeare's women, the self-analyst, has many and divers tones; some of their variety may well be due to the rehandling of the play. A creature of reason and will, she concentrates both on a purpose that is deeper rooted than reason; and the smallest acquaintance with life forbids us to marvel at her choice of a Bertram. Yet she holds her feeling, as if at arm's length, and watches it, even in public. As her reward for curing the king she has to pick her husband from the company of young nobles. Her speech is no mere conceit, it is gravely uttered:

Please it your majesty, I have done already;
The blushes in my cheeks thus whisper me,
'We blush that thou shouldst choose; but, be refused,
Let the white death sit on thy cheek for ever;
We'll ne'er come there again.'

Simple the language is, but not so the idea; the
blushes, which are real enough and honest, have
voices; and we think how, at moments of tension,
Shakespeare ever loves to personify.  His vision of
Helena's introspective nature dictates the peculiar
figure.  The climactic image,

Let the white death sit on thy cheek for ever,

with its rise and fall of sound and hardly definable
image, projects that image before her as in a mirror.
The three emphatic words in the centre of it form,
in Browning's phrase, not a fourth word, but a star.
Here again is the effect, if not the result, of studious
art.

## VI

But to glance, however hastily, at the general
course of Shakespeare's style.  Only a few bearings
can be taken here, and whole regions of the map
must be left out.  I will say little of the narrative
poems; he had already commenced dramatist, and
they are in a sense a by-product.  Some of the
sonnets, to judge by their ruling idea, seem to be of
the same date.  *Venus and Adonis* and the *Rape of
Lucrece* are in a fashion of the hour; in the Ovidian,

Italianate, decorative manner which Marlowe had practised and which Drayton and others were to follow. With their want of shape, their squandering of power, and their numberless false notes, and with their energy and melody and recurrent magnificence, they disclose not only a common form but a common cult. It is the cult of beauty; and primarily of the beauty of youth in man and woman. The temper is that of the artist, grouping and posing his models from the life, with the professional intentness, the emotional detachment, of the studio. He may stop awhile to admire and animate his Adonis: 'Pure shame and awed resistance made him fret, Which bred more beauty in his angry eyes'. But the poet turns aside, puts more heart into his sketch of a hunted hare, and, in general, seems to be not greatly moved. Nor is every reader; for though the imagery be hot and sensuous enough, the fire, to invert Milton's phrase, performs the effect of cold. This may be why the poem (I think the remark is Andrew Bradley's) does not, like *Hero and Leander*, satisfy the imagination. The sense of beauty in Shakespeare, and his expression of it, is a topic that would lead far afield indeed, into the world of Spenser, and of the English Renaissance and beyond; and back again to the English landscape, and to Perdita, and to the magic island. In Shakespeare's plays 'loveliness in favour', in woman or man, is seen usually as no separate gift but as the crown of many attributes, race and breeding, wit or valour: a thoroughly aristocratic conception. Troilus, as pictured by Pandarus, is very like the adored youth of the sonnets:

> Have you any eyes? do you know what a man is? Is not birth, beauty, good shape, discourse, manhood, learning, gentleness, virtue, youth, liberality, and such like, the spice and salt that season a man?

For a sketch like this I need not draw upon plays in which Shakespeare's share can reasonably be contested. The verse of the three early comedies, somewhat thin yet sweet and regular, like 'the current that with gentle murmur glides', still reveals, once or twice in each of them, that the true Shakespeare has arrived. Most of the persons are but delicate sketches, or types; yet the force of the situation, at times, brings them to life and endows them with a music that is new in English poetry. In the *Comedy of Errors*, perhaps the earliest of the group, there are the plaints of the jealous Adriana, and of the old Egeon who supposes that he has been disowned to his face by his own son. His outcry might be too piercing for so light a play if we did not know that presently all will be well. The style —of the kind that comes to sustained perfection in the *Dream*—is of the purest; and the verse, though still, and for long afterwards, moving within the bounds of the self-enclosed line, still often runs over freely, the whole period being spoken almost in a breath:

> Not know my voice! O time's extremity,
> Hast thou so crack'd and splitted my poor tongue

In seven short years, that here my only son
Knows not my feeble key of untuned cares?
Though now this grainèd face of mine be hid
In sap-consuming winter's drizzled snow
And all the conduits of my blood froze up,
Yet hath my night of life some memory,
My wasting lamps some fading glimmer left,
My dull deaf ears a little use to hear:
All these old witnesses—I cannot err—
Tell me thou art my son Antipholus.

## VII

Soon and rather suddenly, with Mercutio and
Bottom and Portia, the great population grows, and
with it the voices, ever more distinctive, multiply.
Figures appear like Puck and Shylock, one of them
a world-figure and a proverb, who like Falstaff have
given adjectives to the dictionary. There are still
fainter types, the Lysanders and Salarinos, often
presented in pairs, who keep the action moving and
whom the playwright, not without a hint or two,
leaves it to the players to distinguish. The main
stream of verse-language, in *Romeo and Juliet* often
turbid, runs clear, if not always deep, in the *Dream*
and the *Merchant of Venice*; for there is no reason for
it to be troubled—except once. There is no serious
clash of persons or of passions in fairyland, or at
Belmont. Only the speech of Shylock, and above
all his shattering prose ('Hath not a Jew eyes? . . .'),
strikes into the world of wit and grace, of nobles and
gentry and defaulters; it would kill any meaner
comedy; and for energy of soul and fullness of

26

cadence there is nothing like it in Shakespeare's
prose until he thinks of Hamlet.   It is needless to
recite the riches of the lyrical imagery, rhymed or
unrhymed; Miss Spurgeon has brought out for us
its profusion in the *Dream*; where, as in certain
scenes in Venice, the action passes under the presiding moon and stars.   The shiftings between verse
and prose, and between rhymed heroics and blank
verse and song are, more nicely than ever yet,
enlisted, in order to express a heightening or lower-
ing of mood, be it in the scene or in the speaker.
Rhyme, which the poet was to use less and less
except for special purposes, and which Swinburne
rashly called his 'evil angel', has many dramatic
virtues.   It adds to the slow gravity of Friar
Laurence, choosing amongst his herbs.   In the
wood near Athens, it gives the formal effect of an
old English square dance, as the four lovers, all
much of one pattern, change partners.   Every
one feels the note of solemnity and ritual in the
rhymes, running into stanza, in the meeting of
Romeo and Juliet; and also at their parting, where
they are sprinkled in with a note of omen:

*Jul.*   O, now be gone; more light and light it grows;
*Rom.*   More light and light; more dark and dark our woes.

Many new kinds of language now appear, ever more
individual; in the fairies and rustics, in the Jew, in
Mercutio and the Nurse.   We begin to come on
the almost unnoticed touches by which a character,
with its memories, its past that is outside the play,

is lit up in a few plain words.  The verse is only
just above the pitch of prose in a certain parenthesis
of Juliet's Nurse, when she says of her mistress that

> Come Lammas-eve at night shall she be fourteen.
> Susan and she·—God rest all Christian souls!—
> Were of an age: well, Susan is with God;
> She was too good for me:—but, as I said,
> On Lammas-eve at night shall she be fourteen.

My memory of Mrs. Stirling, in the old Lyceum, is
that here she lowered her voice, spoke absently,
and crossed herself.  Who was Susan?  We know
enough.  Also in this group of plays the pulse rises
with the increase of song or recitative; the *Dream*
ends, like *Comus*, in a run of short and happy rhymes,
the wedding blessing of the sprites upon the mortals.
For some years, while making his chronicle plays,
Shakespeare had little occasion to sing, being busy
with his orators.  Nor did he, for long, fulfil that
promise of high disquisition in verse, which is given
by the defence of poesy and imagination, assigned
to Theseus: a defence, also, by the playwright, of
the play itself, where 'cool reason' is in abeyance.

### VIII

There is less variety of accent in the history plays
that begin with *Richard III*.  Here presides a new
sort of rhetoric, which in that tragedy is loud and
monotonous for all its splendours; while in *Richard
II* it is subtler, full of images drawn out fine as

28

spiders' webs, and of wonderful exercises in melody. The self-pitying king, the only king in Shakespeare who is presented as *consciously* a poet, seems to infect the other speakers, even his gardener, with his habit of speech; which is with him even while he is being stabbed. Almost every one who speaks verse in these Histories is an orator, even in soliloquy. Now begin the grand unfolding of the colours, the fanfare of the vowels, the march of plea and counterplea, in entreaty or invective or self-excuse. The speeches of royalty become ever longer; thirty, forty lines on end. The three in the 'crowning scene' in *Henry IV* reveal, by a new method of presenting character, the whole nature, the pent-up painful confidences, of the father and son. But they are not too long, they rise superbly to a climax. One other trait of these Histories may be noticed. The court and the battlefield, besides the tavern, are their theatre of action; and here there can be no natural scenery before the eyes of the dramatis personæ; no lark at dawn, no moonlit country-side. Yet the images of nature refuse to be left out; they creep, they throng into the speeches—but now, as part of the speaker's passions or emotions, by way of metaphor, and often of formal simile. The eyes of opposed armies are '*like* the meteors of a troubled heaven'; the Welsh lady's song charms the hearer,

> Making such difference 'twixt wake and sleep
> As is the difference betwixt day and night
> The hour before the heavenly-harness'd team
> Begins his golden progress in the east.

29

In the vext mind of Henry of Lancaster, the images
kindle one another [n] like sparks in a train, and the
troubled style of the later tragedies is in sight:

> O God! that one might read the book of fate,
> And see the revolution of the times
> Make mountains level, and the continent,
> Weary of solid firmness, melt itself
> Into the sea! and, other times, to see
> The beachy girdle of the ocean
> Too wide for Neptune's hips! how chances mock,
> And changes fill the cup of alteration
> With divers liquors!   O, if this were seen,
> The happiest youth, viewing his progress through,
> What perils past, what crosses to ensue,
> Would shut the book, and sit him down and die.

All things are in flux: the vision of the earth flattened,
then melted into the sea, calls up that of the sea itself,
with the god straddling neck-high as in the old
maps of the *Poly-Olbion*; the image of a liquid
persists, but now it is only a bitter cupful; the
abstract words 'revolution', 'alteration', enforce the
sense of change; and then the intellect, ceasing
to drift on these dreams, pulls itself up, remembers
its original image, and closes with the book of fate
once more.   Such a process of thought can be
traced a hundred times afterwards, in the tragedies;
indeed Henry the Fourth, with his baffled wish to
expiate his offence by a pilgrimage, has the makings
of a tragic hero.   He is more interesting than his
son, who is so often called, and truly, the poet's presentment of a pattern king, a champion of England

and also at one in spirit with his people. He, too, in his speech on the idol Ceremony, so much more moving than his public and martial trumpetings, is a master of the magnificent style, with its 'intertissued robe of gold and pearl'; and yet it is less poignant than are the musings of his father. Shakespeare, we may feel, had been waiting to find a language, lofty and above all sustained, that should beseem a king who was after his own heart; but there was nothing in John, or in the two Richards, that could evoke it. Now he achieves it; and presently, as though he had made the utmost of it, he drops it, with its special pageantry and colouring; and he turns to Rome, and legendary Denmark, and legendary Britain, there to find a dialect for the harsher problems of the will and conscience.

IX

His other achievement, about the turn of the century, in these history plays and the comedies that interlace them, is to create a new prose, for a new world that speaks in prose. Here, as Dr. Johnson said of Charing Cross, we are in the full tide of human existence. As to the graver prose, now so much enriched, and often alternating with verse on the lips of the same speaker, it is found in *Hamlet* and in *Henry the Fifth*, and is no less deeply inspired than their poetry. In the case of Henry, its use is plainly dictated by the fundamental conception of his character. He talks with his people, with Bates

31

and Williams, in their own language: they do not know who he is:

> The king is but a man, as I am: the violet smells to him as it doth to me; the element shows to him as it doth to me; all his senses have but human conditions; his ceremonies laid by, in his nakedness he appears but a man. . . .

The other aspect of man, as he is or may be, 'the beauty of the world, the paragon of animals', is also proclaimed, in Hamlet's, in Shakespeare's, greatest piece of prose.   Hamlet says that the picture cannot delight *him*, but plainly it delights Shakespeare. At the other extreme is the speech of Falstaff and his circle; and this continues, somewhat dulled except for the description of his death, in the humours of Nym and Pistol, caricature-types.   The mere verbal stores of Falstaff and the peculiar rhetoric of his wit would demand a long description; let me only note the strength of his observing intellect, which comes out best of all in his soliloquies as in his picture of his ragged regiment, 'the cankers of a calm world and a long peace', the 'tattered prodigals lately come from swine-keeping'.   We know, too, of his easy, his profane acquaintance with the language of scripture and the tones of the pulpit, and, at some time in the past, with the 'inside of a church'.   Shylock's allusions had been to the Old Testament.

X

I am omitting the 'middle comedies', on which so much could be said to the purpose, in order to touch on two or three features of the great tragedies. Each of them has its own pervading and distinctive style, deriving from the content. But consider the general quality that culminates in their language, the quality of *grandeur*. It is a word not easy to define with any precision; and I will avoid the difficult æsthetic problem that is raised by the kind of grandeur which seems to be almost denuded of beauty—the kind that is abundant in the play of *Coriolanus*.

The veteran critics, Matthew Arnold [n] and George Saintsbury,[n] were fond of speaking, though in very different senses, of the 'grand style' in poetry. Matthew Arnold used to hand us passages from Homer, Virgil, or Milton, which we were to keep as touchstones, and which were bound, if we applied them, to show up all inferior metal. He quoted the noblest lines that he could think of; and most of them, as we should expect from him, though not all, have some kind of high ethical suggestion, as in Milton's lines,

> Standing on earth, not rapt above the pole,
> Mor safe I sing, with mortal voice, unchang'd
> To hoarse or mute, though fall'n on evil days,
> On evil days though fall'n, and evil tongues.

This counsel of Matthew Arnold's is not outworn;

but we are looking for a particular species, the dramatic species, of the style. Saintsbury, ever more flexible and generous in his admirations and loth to think of any kind of perfection as higher or lower than another, goes to the other extreme, and finds the grand style more easily; in what he calls the 'central splendour of Adriana's speech' in the *Errors*, or in the tirades of Timon. Again we need not quarrel, except to plead that though these things are magnificent, and also dramatic, no word seems to be left for something that is greater yet. I would suggest letting the phrase 'the grand style' take care of itself, and keeping to the noun 'grandeur', which in our usage means something more; and also, in the case of a dramatist, limiting it by the word 'dramatic'. Poetry, in a play, may have philosophical grandeur without being specially dramatic; like the speech of Ulysses on order, or some of the superb Stoical passages in the tragedies of Chapman. But the words of Ajax, though they come in an epic, have dramatic grandeur: 'Slay me, but so it be in the light.' They are referred to by the great critic known as 'Longinus' [n]; and he insists that the highest effects of style can only be won when they are 'the echo' (or reverberation) 'of a great soul'. Longinus, however, takes most of his instances from non-dramatic verse or from prose oratory. For the quality we seek, I suggest that the great soul must be speaking at some crisis of its fate, with the whole force of the story behind it and in our mind; be it at the crisis of a conflict

34

or decision, or in the moment when this conflict is resolved and the speaker bids farewell to life, or to all hope in life; and does so in words which alone beseem the occasion. Poetical grandeur is thus the genus, dramatic grandeur the species. This last is hardly present, for instance, in the famed lines of Claudio in *Measure for Measure* on the after-life, 'Aye, but to die, and go we know not where.' True, they are dramatic in so far as Claudio is condemned to die, and is pleading for his life; but there is not the great nature or the strong action, the true dramatic energy, behind them. So, too, with the words of Hotspur, sublime as they are, and the utmost that Shakespeare had so far achieved in this kind. Burke, in his discussion of the 'sublime', argues that one of its characteristics is in some way to suggest infinity; and Hotspur exclaims

> But thought's the slave of life, and life time's fool;
> And time, that takes survey of all the world,
> Must have a stop.

Shakespeare, before he wrote *Julius Cæsar*, seldom gives us anything like this, for the good reason that he had thought of no personage sufficiently great, and placed in a situation sufficiently great, to beget such utterance. In the major tragedies, dramatic grandeur, while in a sense pervasive, is most marked in the actual valedictions, Macbeth's 'To-morrow, and to-morrow, and to-morrow', and in Othello's 'Soft you; a word or two before you go.' But dramatic grandeur of language need not culminate

35

in a single peak.    In *Lear* there is range over range,
each one of which we had thought to be the last.
Lear is called upon not to decide on action but to
realize the truth; and this process is gradual.    We
can hardly fix on any one moment or acme, unless
we choose 'What, have his daughters brought him
to this pass?'    Perhaps, in *King Lear*, the dramatic
grandeur is at its height wherever the expression
of personal suffering is united with the highest
metaphysical style; which deals in universals, and
is here employed in judgement upon the whole
disorder of this impious world: as in the king's
invocations to the indifferent gods, or in

> Take physic, pomp;
> Expose thyself to feel what wretches feel,
> That thou mayst shake the superflux to them,
> And show the heavens more just.


### XI

*Julius Cæsar*, with which the tragic period opens,
every one feels to be simply and lucidly composed,
and to show what Dowden calls the perfect balance
between thought and expression.    Deceptively, perhaps, as regards the thought.    The play may
remind us of the saying, I think of Goethe, that
Shakespeare lays character and motive before us like
the exposed works of a watch.    Yes, but which of
us here can understand, though he may behold, the
works of a watch?    I cannot; nor have I ever
grasped the thought, or ruling idea, of *Julius Cæsar*.

## Style in Shakespeare

In any case, as time passes, the style becomes progressively (we must not say, in a straight line, for many of our dates are uncertain, but still becomes) stranger, darker, richer in vocabulary, more intricate in construction, and in metre not only freer, but at last so near to the patternless rhythm of prose, that we begin to tax the poet with some loss of respect for his instrument. This process has often been described. Dowden speaks of a 'preponderance or excess of the ideas over the means of giving them utterance', of the 'rapid and abrupt turnings of thought', and of the 'impatient activity of intellect and fancy' which cannot stop to work out an idea. But let me quote from the words, too little known save to students, of a young Aberdonian of a century ago. They occur in James Spalding's [n] *Letter on Shakespeare's Authorship of 'The Two Noble Kinsmen'*, in the course of a comparison with the style of John Fletcher:

> He abounds in hinted descriptions, in sketches of imagery, in abrupt and vanishing snatches of fancy. . . . Everywhere his incessant activity and quickness, both of intellect and fancy, engaged him in a continual struggle with speech; it is a sluggish slave which he would force to a burden beyond its strength; a weary courser which he would urge at a speed to which it is unequal . . . it is the excess of strength which hurts, not weakness which incapacitates. . . . He has impressed no other of his own mental qualities on all his characters; this quality colours every one of them. It is one to which poetry is apt to give a very subordinate place. . . . Imagination is active, powerfully and unceasingly; but she is rebuked by the presence of a mightier influence; she

37

is but the handmaid of the active and piercing intellect . . .
crowding thoughts and fancies into the narrowest space, and
submitting to obscurity in preference to feeble dilation.

We need but think of 'To be or not to be', or of
Coriolanus at his angriest, to see the pertinence of
this description. It covers, however, many differences and extremes of craftsmanship, from the
recurring harshness of *Timon of Athens* to the unexcelled harmonies of *Antony and Cleopatra*; a play
in which, as Sir Edmund Chambers remarks, we
may feel that the balance between thought and
expression is recovered. But there is certainly the
further question: Trying to shun both pedantry and
idolatry, what are we to *think* of this troubled way
of writing? Is it not, again and again, simply
bad?—not to be explained by any corruption in the
text, or to be dramatically justified by any distraction
or turbulence in the speaker. It is best to admit
the regret. Quotation would be unpleasing; one
can open, in *Coriolanus* [n] for instance, on twenty lines,
made up of two sentences full of thorny grammar
and confusions. To-day in every high school it is
taught, and to every examiner the lament is proffered,
that Shakespeare's blank metre, with its weightless
line-endings, often tends to lose its pattern. These
may be amongst the thousand things which Ben
Jonson wished to have been blotted. I speak of
course of cases where the text cannot reasonably be
questioned. They are extreme instances of the
new, intellectualized style which Shakespeare was
led to invent by his conception of heroic character,

and of racking situation. We cannot decide whether, as some have guessed (knowing perhaps more about Shakespeare than did his maker), any disturbing personal experience lies behind his tragedies. Of course, and despite all excesses, this new style *is*, in general, supremely dramatic: the native and predestined expression of Lear on the heath, or of Timon with his gold; no need to emphasize its endless variety, or its ever-fresh revelations of the power of sound. Developed for the utterance of tragic discord, it becomes ever more close-packed, elliptical, and strange or difficult, not to say inharmonious. And yet, in one play at least, *Antony and Cleopatra*, there is a certain exultation of spirit, which begets a rhythm ever more buoyant and magical, and which derives directly from Shakespeare's transfiguring of the personages he found in his Plutarch. Few can feel in *Macbeth* or *Othello* that the ending leaves us with the sense that the chief actors have triumphed over their destiny. But in *Antony and Cleopatra* that impression is enforced by the very beat of the lines, by the fall of the changing pauses and by the peculiar soar of the language:

> For his bounty,
> There was no winter in't; an autumn 'twas
> That grew the more by reaping: his delights
> Were dolphin-like; they show'd his back above
> The element they lived in: in his livery
> Walk'd crowns and crownets, realms and islands were
> As plates dropp'd from his pocket.

XII

This rich and uplifted style is prophetic; for, with its wildness tempered down, it is heard, with its unmistakable tune, in the Romances that were soon to follow. I will mention but one feature of them. Here, as we know, tragedy is merely threatened, and its logic is suspended; since the poet, for reasons that are hid from us, now prefers, as though by an arbitrary turn of the wrist, to stave off disaster, and to close with a scene of unalloyed beauty; like that which released the spirit of the offending Ancient Mariner as he watched the water-snakes. Now in the *Winter's Tale* and in *Cymbeline* there is the definitely ethical element; there is free forgiveness, and oblivion of all errors. But, once, this element is absent, namely in Shakespeare's contribution to the play of *Pericles*. The scene is one of recognition, pure and simple, with no real *drama* behind it; as is the case in many a medieval romance, and in the tradition of the far-travelled story of Apollonius of Tyre. I would call this an example, not excelled, of Shakespeare's refreshed, and purged, and final style, now bare and now opulent, in which his most favoured technical resources are at easy command. Pericles lies in a stupor on the ship; and his daughter Marina, supposed to be lost, charms him awake and gradually reveals her identity. She has been bitterly tried, but has come out of the trials with dignity; she is a woman, not a young girl; and she begins in a

weighty, even manner, with long words from the
Latin, not unlike that of the English Histories:

> Though wayward fortune did malign my state,
> My derivation was from ancestors
> Who stood equivalent with mighty kings . . .

Presently the pace quickens, the lines are freely
divided between the speakers, and the words are of
the easiest:

*Mar.* Patience, good sir,
Or here I'll cease.
*Per.* Nay, I'll be patient.
Thou little know'st how thou dost startle me
To call thyself Marina.
*Mar.* The name
Was given me by one that had some power;
My father, and a king.

But as the facts dawn upon Pericles, simplicity is not
enough for him. As I said, the poet, at the height
of an action, loves to personify—a process that in
its nature carries the emotion beyond the occasion,
and tends to universalize it. Pericles can find no
words for his daughter but to compare her to
'Patience gazing on kings' graves, and smiling
Extremity out of act', or to 'a palace For the crown'd
truth to dwell in'. Yet the finale is plain again:

> O, come hither,
> Thou that beget'st him that did thee beget;

and, later:

> Give me my robes. I am wild in my beholding.

Still but half himself, he seems to hear heavenly music, and he concludes, 'Let me rest.' Thus the style that was originally inspired by the need of expressing tragic grandeur retains its virtue, and its actual movement, when adapted to express pure happiness.

Some one must have thought of the parallel before; but here another of the great recognition-scenes of literature comes to mind; I mean, in the *Electra* [n] of Sophocles. True, the *Electra* is a tragedy of blood and retribution; but this is awhile forgotten in the inserted idyll. Orestes returns to avenge his father and to kill his murderess-mother and her partner. Electra had sent him away, while yet a boy, for safety. He has spread the report that he is dead; and he appears before her as a stranger, a grown man, carrying the urn that is supposed to hold his ashes. Here, as in *Pericles*, the disclosure is long and delicately led up to, so that the shock of happiness may not be sudden; here, too, grace and beauty rule, without loss of strength; and the words of Electra, when she knows the truth, are brief: 'What, art *thou* he?' and 'O voice, hast thou come?' and Orestes says, 'Let no other voice reply.' The art of Shakespeare and that of the antique, as is often said, can be near akin. I have assumed, as calling for no argument, that my hearers share in the semi-mystical view of style, indeed of all artistic creation, which I have implied throughout. Work which way you will, up from the dictionary, or downward from the poet's conception, the two

42

processes can never meet; at the centre, there is always something insoluble. You cannot combine the results of analysis by any nameable process of adding up, or of attempted fusion, and so explain what could never have been predicted. Philosophers have found the blessed word 'emergent' to indicate, or to disguise, their complete ignorance of the unknown factor, the $x$, which is implied in the transition from dead matter to life, or from life to mind. Perfect expression, too, is such an emergent; and to detect its secret would ask for a superhuman intelligence.

# The Present Value of Byron

The title, commercial as it sounds, is suggested
by the centenary, now (1924) being celebrated,
of Byron's death.    What can be meant, at any time,
by the 'present value' of a poet?    It is not to be
measured by sales and editions, or by the pious
passing glow of enthusiasm that is kindled by the
occasion.    After all, it comes down to each one of
us asking, What is Byron to *me?*    To 'me and
many other mes', according to the old Oxford
rhyme; but, in the long run, to *this* 'me'.    And that
we shall find out best by reading Byron through
again, rather than by reading what better judges
than ourselves have said about him.    Never mind
if he was cursed when alive for his bad morals, and
after his death for his bad prosody.    Let us try to
get our own impressions pure.    Above all, let us
forget all that we ourselves may have written concerning him.    Let us go over him once more and
ask how far our confused young ardours and dislikes are wearing now.    Criticism, possibly, is
partly the attempt to recover these first inarticulate
feelings, and to understand them; the result may be

worth more than the mature official judgement which has been overlaid by much reading or teaching. This, no doubt, is not exactly a Wordsworthian view of the 'intimations' of our early years. The starting-point is that old, unpurged, Galignani Byron which somehow had got on to the school shelves. What about it now? I will only try to answer a few simple questions and will deal very little in literary history or in eulogy.

I have always felt that Byron's future is safe, not only with critics, and not only with persons who care for poetry, but with persons who do not much care for it at all. This may sound a double-edged saying, but it is well intended. It implies, for one thing, that the man, apart from his writings, can never be forgotten, just as Swift, Johnson, and Carlyle can never be forgotten, whatever becomes, in the judgement of Time, of their formal works. I choose these names because they are the English writers of mark whom we know best personally; and Byron we know in the same way. All four have told us an immense amount about themselves, and others have told us almost more about them. Over the other three Byron has at least one advantage: he has spoken of himself, and at great length, both in his best prose and in his best verse. I have met various people who have very little sense for literature but who could not keep away from Byron. Mr. Murray, writing some time ago, spoke of the stream of pilgrims who come to see his Byron museum. For the man is still an enigma, although the broad lines of his character are familiar. Nor does the interest in Byron depend upon unsolved scandals, which so far as I am concerned may go down to their own place in the gutter. It is doubtful whether after all they throw any but an indirect light upon his poetry. Nor, again, does the interest depend on any 'message', or deep philosophical idea, that Byron can furnish. It depends on his mixed and large humanity, on his way of continually disappointing us, and of suddenly recovering himself and triumphing.

## II

The first, then, of my questions is this: *Can he tell a story?* The gift of narrative is of course not the same as the poetic gift. The two things *may* go together; but they need not, in mathematical language, vary together. Even when they go together, as in Chaucer and William Morris they do, they are still different. Gower, Chaucer's friend, is something of a poet, but he is much more of a tale-teller; and his narrative ease carries him through when his poetry wears thin. When Shelley tries to tell a tale, his poetic gift just carries him through when the narrative wears thin. As to Byron, he begins very ill in this particular, and for a long time he does not improve at all; but at last he disappoints us pleasantly. His series of lays, poured out so fast, and so wildly successful at the time, are mostly, as stories, poor things, not only in subject but in treatment. The *Giaour*, he said himself, was but a string of passages. The *Bride of Abydos* is an anecdote. In the *Corsair* there is a tale, but it is swamped in declamation. The *Siege of Corinth*, with its rough but not ineffective variations on the subtle rhythms of *Christabel*, has a splendid descriptive energy. The picture of the siege lives; but there is not much of a story. In *Parisina* something does happen; there is at least one tragic moment; it is the most genuine of all these early tales; and there is a note of high-strained but sincere pathos. *The Prisoner of Chillon* does not profess to be a story, except for the slow tortures of the dungeon. In all these poems there is a great momentum, a profusion of rhetorical and passionate matter, which is rather dull to-day, and a half-pennyworth of story. Byron's lays displaced those of Scott in the ear of the many; and Scott, in his modest way, accepted the finding of the many; too modestly; for his own lays, I think, wear far better than most of Byron's. His picture of Flodden and his *Lord of the Isles* leave a far more satisfactory and distinct impression; and, as the sequel was to show, he was a tale-teller born. But Byron had not come to the end of his tether. He got these lays behind him, and then he discovered a better form of narrative. And he discovered it the moment that he brought to bear, or rather that he ceased to forgo, his gift of humour, of irony, and of portraying real life. This change is evident in *Mazeppa*, written while he was already deep in *Don Juan*.

*Mazeppa*, as a poem, and also as a tale, is alive.
There is not only the speed and magnificence of the
ride, in which Scott for once is matched on Scott's
own ground, but there is the light vivacity of the
setting:

> There was a certain Palatine,
>     A count of far and high descent,
> Rich as a salt or silver mine;
> And he was proud, ye may divine,
>     As if from heaven he had been sent;
> He had such wealth in blood and ore
>     As few could match beneath the throne;
> And he would gaze upon his store,
> And o'er his pedigree would pore,
>     Until by some confusion led,
>     Which almost look'd like want of head,
> He thought their merits were his own.
> His wife was not of his opinion;
> His junior she by thirty years,
> Grew daily tired of his dominion. . . .

And in the same strain the story closes.   Mazeppa
has been telling it to the fugitive Charles XII,
after the battle of Pultowa, under an oak tree:

> And if ye marvel Charles forgot
> To thank his tale, *he* wonder'd not,—
> The king had been an hour asleep.

In form, *Mazeppa* is still a lay; but meanwhile, as
we know, Byron had hit on quite a different method
of story-telling.   It was the old, discursive, ironical
Italian method.   *Beppo* is his gay little first adventure of this kind.   It is another anecdote: the
husband, long thought to be lost, comes home in

the guise of a Turk; introduces himself, with polite-
ness and tact, to his wife and to his successor, and
all goes smoothly. That is the whole; all the virtue
is in the embroidery, in the arabesque; and these
are perfect. Such, too, is the method of *Don Juan*,
with its flow of wit, vulgarity—even flat boorishness
—confession, observation, colour, and poetry. That
poem is a great and permanent landmark in the
progress of a particular form; here Byron rivals his
forerunners, from Pulci to Casti, and their successors
to whom they gave an impulse, in France, in Spain,
and in Russia. For De Musset, for Espronceda,
for Pushkin, that form comes through Byron, with
the stamp that Byron set upon it; it does not come
directly from the Italian originals. Some of them,
like the author of *Evgeny Onegin*, restored a certain
plastic delicacy of which Byron was incapable.
He aims, far more violently than do his models
(amongst whom we must reckon Frere with his
pleasant *Whistlecraft*) at producing a continual sense
of shock and discord, as much by his sudden soarings
into poetry as by his more frequent and sudden
drops into anticlimax. Further, Byron's habit is to
let his mind and story drift—drift back to himself,
and then swiftly away again to the subject. And
these traits distinguish him also from Chaucer;
who embroiders indeed and digresses, but who
leaves a sense of harmony and not of discord; and,
who, when he speaks of himself from time to time,
speaks gently, and not for long. There is, of
course, the other old Italian way of narrative, which is

seen in the prose of the *Decameron* and its successors.
Here the teller keeps out of sight, and the story is
stripped down to its naked perfection. There is
something of this quality in Byron's letters, when
he briefly portrays a scene, or recites a scandal.

Byron rises to his full power as a narrator when
the tale itself provides the irony, and he feels that
he need not comment much; when he can go slowly
and delightedly from pageant to pageant, inter-
spersing dialogue in verse, a form in which he can
be a master, and showing, what in his dramas he
does not show, his dramatic power. The familiar
fifth canto of *Don Juan* is as good an instance as
another. Juan is taken into the slave-market at
Constantinople, has a long talk with an older
Englishman, who is also on sale; is carried in female
dress to the Sultana Gulbeyaz who has caught sight
of him, and repels her advances; begins to relent,
but is saved just in time by the appearance of the
Sultan. The old attendant gives warning:

'Bride of the Sun! and Sister of the Moon!'
 ('Twas thus he spake,) 'and Empress of the Earth!
Whose frown would put the spheres all out of tune,
 Whose smile makes all the planets dance with mirth,
Your slave brings tidings—he hopes not too soon—
 Which your sublime attention may be worth:
The Sun himself has sent me like a ray,
To hint that he is coming up this way.'

'Is it,' exclaimed Gulbeyaz, 'as you say?
 I wish to heaven he would not shine till morning!
But bid my women form the Milky-way.
 Hence, my old comet! give the stars due warning—

And, Christian! mingle with them as you may,
   And as you'd have me pardon your past scorning'—
Here they were interrupted by a humming
Sound, and then by a cry, 'The Sultan's coming!'

Here are the qualities that Goethe liked so well, in
*Don Juan* and in *The Vision of Judgment*—the
nimbleness, the daring, the impudence, the light-
someness; and that strain is kept up through 159
stanzas, of which about thirty, here and there, can
fairly be called digressive; nor do these come too
thick when once the story is set going. Byron is
much better when he thus moves free of any docu-
ments, sailing buoyantly along. Even the digressions reveal *him* to us. Just at the start, he
breaks off for seven verses to describe a sight he
had seen while actually writing the canto—a man,
the commandant, lying ferociously killed, shot dead,
in the streets of Ravenna; this event he describes,
in his terse prose, in a letter. The best parts of
*Don Juan* run thus easily. Often enough the tale
is of choicer fabric than the patched-in comment.
In this sense, then, Byron takes his rank among the
four or five best English story-tellers in rhyme,
from Chaucer to Crabbe, and onwards.

### III

My second question is this: *Could Byron sing?*
The world for a long time thought so; he sang of
himself, and the world thought the subject a good
one; and Goethe thought so too, when he said that

his Euphorion, who is Byron, had 'a song his very own'—*ein eigenster Gesang*. But it is doubtful whether Goethe was thinking there of strictly lyrical power; he may have been referring to Byron's general poetic gift. And besides, even a great poet may be fallible about the quality of a lyric gift in a language that is not his own. And then Europe, we remember, from Portugal to Sweden, from Athens to Moscow, mostly read Byron in translation; the library, the mere bibliography, of those translations and of the imitations they bred, can scarcely yet have been catalogued, still less reviewed, as a whole. In England, as we know, the next two generations of poets began to cast doubt on the purity of Byron's poetic gift, long before the rest of the world had done so. The criticism of Matthew Arnold, and his contrast of Leopardi with Byron as a poetic artist, cuts deep; and the still louder disgust of Swinburne, who was a sound judge, when he spoke of Byron's dissonances, was founded in truth. I shall not waste time by going over that ground; we know pretty well by now what Byron, in the way of song, could *not* give; we know all about his lapses of ear, about the deadly commonness that intrudes so often even into his lyric; and to know this is no credit to us, who have heard these critics, and whose ears have been sharpened by familiarity with Shelley and other artists who are finer than Byron. But what is it in lyric that Byron can and does give us? This is not so easy to define, but I will try. We need only

take him at his best. His best is what it is, and is
not affected by the fact that he could be very bad
at other times.

We all know the handful of good lyrics that
Palgrave saved for his *Golden Treasury*; and Palgrave's comment helps us to an answer, though I
will put it in my own way. Creature of moods,
and chameleon, as Byron was, he was not a child
of the eighteenth century for nothing. And in the
long run, I believe that what we get down to in
him is an eighteenth-century characteristic: I mean,
the ascendancy of *reason*. I shall press this point
again; but meantime, he does one of the hardest
of things: at his best, he reasons in song, and that
without ceasing to sing. Song is winged, no doubt,
by feeling; but he reasons *about* feeling. He keeps
firmly to his thread; he is a master of the logic of
feeling, which is not the logic of the mere understanding. He reasons about grief, and estrange-
ment, and his tortured heart, and his absence, and
his exile. And it is when he does this, and does
it sincerely—sincerely, at least, for the moment, and
that is all that is required—it is then, I say, that his
lyrical gift is purest, his phrase most piercing, and
his rhythm safest. No matter whether his Thyrza
is a real or an imaginary woman. The evidence,
on his own word, is that she was real, though we
are not sure who she was. Only one, the noblest
and most perfect, of his Thyrza poems is very widely
known; it is in all the books: 'And thou art dead,
as young and fair.' It is a masterpiece of thinking

about sorrow, and it is in style as pure as anything
in Shelley; and it has more shape, it is more definite
and plastic, and leaves a deeper dint on the mind,
than almost anything in Shelley; though it must
lose, no doubt, by the absence of such an *aura*, or
spray of suggestion, as Shelley communicates to
his frailest lyrics. There is little of that element in
it; nothing is left unsaid; but then, how much is
said! I quote, in illustration, from another Thyrza
piece, 'Without a stone to mark the spot', which is
far less perfect as a whole:

> And didst thou not, since Death for thee
>  Prepared a light and pangless dart,
> Once long for him thou ne'er shalt see,
>  Who held, and holds thee in his heart?
>
> Oh! who like him had watched thee here?
>  Or sadly mark'd thy glazing eye,
> In that dread hour ere death appear,
>  When silent sorrow fears to sigh,
>
> Till all was past?

This, in tone and temper, is unlike most of our
romantic verse. The strain is older, and can, I
think, be traced back into the age which is falsely
supposed to be unpoetical and dispassionate. It
has the finish and the inscriptional effect that we
associate with our so-called classical period. Do we
not sometimes hear in Byron an echo of Rochester?
I have often thought that Byron, at his best, might
have written some of Rochester's best things; al-

though, it is true, Rochester had more to repent of than Byron, and repented more deeply, and his few singing arrows go home more surely than anything of Byron's; but the affinity is there:

> When, weary'd with a world of woe,
>   To thy safe bosom I retire,
> Where Love, and Peace, and Truth does flow,
>   May I contented there expire. . . .

Byron may not rise to that; but in recompense, he has his gift of impassioned reasoning in connected soliloquy, which is not the less spontaneous for all its logic, and which we feel kindling as it proceeds; it is not thought out beforehand.   More than this, he sometimes catches a true song-tune, and shows a musical craft not unlike that of his friend Moore. Would any man who was destitute of this craft have shortened by a foot the last line in the following eight?

> For the sword outwears its sheath,
>   And the soul wears out the breast,
> And the heart must pause to breathe,
>   And love itself have rest.
>
> Though the night was made for loving,
>   And the day returns too soon,
> Yet we'll go no more a-roving
>   By the light of the moon.

Even in the *Hours of Idleness*, his *péché de jeunesse*, and still more in *Hebrew Melodies* ('Oh! snatch'd away in Beauty's bloom'), and most of all, perhaps, in the three or four poems 'To Augusta', this rarer strain is heard. And the most musical of these has, again, an eighteenth-century measure and melody, the melody of Gray's *Amatory Stanzas* and of Cowper's 'The poplars are felled'. The passionate or affectionate matter is kept in order and solemnized by the restraint and balance of that good tradition. The second verse rises, no doubt, above the first, which is cast in antitheses. I know it is in the anthologies, but it will bear repeating:

> Though human, thou didst not deceive me,
>   Though woman, thou didst not forsake,
> Though loved, thou forborest to grieve me,
>   Though slander'd, thou never couldst shake;
> Though trusted, thou didst not disclaim me,
>   Though parted, it was not to fly,
> Though watchful, 'twas not to defame me,
>   Nor, mute, that the world might belie. . . .
>
> From the wreck of the past, which hath perish'd,
>   Thus much I at least may recall,
> It hath taught me that what I most cherish'd
>   Deserv'd to be dearest of all;
> In the desert a fountain is springing,
>   In the wide waste there still is a tree,
> And a bird in the solitude singing,
>   Which speaks to my spirit of *thee*.

It is not perfect, with its snags in the syntax and rhythm; yet the poets who have criticized Byron might have been proud to sign it. It is needless to speak of his other, his martial strain, of the *Isles of Greece* and kindred pieces. They have all his *vivida vis*, but seem to be of a lower and louder kind of poetry, which has its own rights, no doubt; but they suffer at once when confronted with the sublimer note of Shelley in *his* mood of patriot or humanitarian ardour:

> The world's great age begins anew,
> The golden years return:

To that ineffable, or transcendental, note Byron cannot rise. But for all that he has a 'song his very own'.

IV

My third question, which is partly the same as the second, is this: *What has Byron to say to our sense of beauty?* What kind of feeling has he for beauty—visible beauty—and how far does he manage to get it into his language? Here we are embarrassed by the fact that he came to be more and more ashamed of his feeling, and that it is part of his method, latterly, to interrupt in a brutal way his expression of his feeling. He pours out mockeries and vulgarities and squalors and anticlimaxes in the same breath, when he is describing something or somebody lovely. Here, no doubt, he is true to himself, and it is all part of his repertory of tricks; but we need not feel that we are sentimental, if we are sometimes indignant. It is as though Byron could not fix his gaze for long at a time on what is well and fair. One of the old-fashioned reviewers put this point when he remarked that Byron aims 'at what we must term the *suicidal success* of extinguishing in laughter the refined emotions he had raised'. I shall not give examples, which are on every page. But we must not count amongst these interruptions such gay, human, and corrective passages as temper the idyll of Juan and Haidee. That, surely, in point of clean plastic beauty and harmonious execution, is still Byron's masterpiece. I do not understand, after reading it again, why some good critics deny to Byron any quality of greatness. Here he is simple, natural, and sincere; the bathing, the handmaid cooking the eggs and coffee, the young sculptured figures who live in the moment—all this is as well done, I dare to say, in verse as that other idyll of Richard Feverel and Lucy is done in prose;—in a prose which, as has more than once been said, is crying out to become verse. Byron's feeling for external beauty is doubtless not of the subtlest, but it is strong. Nothing is intimate, unearthly, speculative, little is left to the imagination; he sets to work our realizing faculty, and makes us see, not dream. I will not quote the description of the couple wandering 'over the shining pebbles and the shells', it is too familiar; and so is the picture of the sleepers in the harem. Less known is that of the English mansion, 'Norman Abbey', in the thirteenth canto of *Don Juan*:

> It stood embosom'd in a happy valley,
>     Crown'd by high woodlands, where the Druid oak
> Stood, like Caractacus, in act to rally
>     His host, with broad arms 'gainst the thunderstroke,

And from beneath his boughs were seen to sally
   The dappled foresters; as day awoke,
The branching stag swept down with all his herd,
To quaff a brook which murmur'd like a bird.

Before the mansion lay a lucid lake,
   Broad as transparent, deep, and freshly fed
By a river, which its soften'd way did take
   In currents by the calmer water spread
Around: the wildfowl nestled in the brake
   And sedges, brooding in their liquid bed:
The woods sloped downwards to its brink, and stood
With their green faces fix'd upon the flood. . . .

Any one can pick holes in this; would Tennyson
have allowed the jingle *Caractacus . . . act?* Or *did
take?* No, he would not. But stand a little way
back, and the broad, free composition tells, and the
effect is beautiful. Byron's plastic sense was not,
we may think, originally strong; but his wanderings
among the galleries of painting and sculpture,
which he describes so rhetorically in *Childe Harold*,
may well have sharpened it.

### v

But what of his instinct for beauty and harmony
in *language?* We have been told for fifty years
what a sinner he is in this respect; and we all know
how bad he can be, and how bad he seems to wish
to be. No one to-day, perhaps, cares much for
the breathless iteration of pseudo-passionate matter
which charmed the first readers of his lays. But let
us take Byron when we know that he is in earnest—

at least for the moment—and where no irony can intrude. It may seem strange to compare him with Wordsworth, whom he both mocked at and venerated. But sometimes he commands a clear and pure fount of diction, one or two degrees above grave prose, which is curiously like Wordsworth's diction. Byron could often inspire his words with beauty when his feeling itself ran clear and pure. I find this diction in *The Dream*. Here he imagines, or remembers, how in the hour of his wedding to Miss Milbanke he found himself thinking of Mary Chaworth. The lines will be known here in Nottingham, and to this audience, better than anywhere else; but I quote a few of them to bear out my suggestion that in diction they are Wordsworthian; whether consciously or not is another matter:

> And he stood calm and quiet, and he spoke
> The fitting vows, but heard not his own words,
> And all things reel'd around him; he could see
> Not that which was, nor that which should have been—
> But the old mansion, and the accustom'd hall,
> And the remember'd chambers, and the place,
> The day, the hour, the sunshine, and the shade;
> All things pertaining to that place and hour,
> And her who was his destiny,—came back
> And thrust themselves between him and the light:
> What business had they there at such a time?

The last line, considered as poetry, is audacious; but I think that it stands, and that it clinches the whole. Byron's blank verse has been so much and so justly raked and scarified that we welcome this musical strain, caught in a happy moment when his ear and his heart were honest.

But if we enlarge our question regarding beauty, and ask whether Byron can also give us grandeur of language, or what in his age was still called the Sublime, we must go carefully. This quality we should expect to find, if anywhere, in the *Cain* which Goethe admired so highly. And a certain grandeur of conception in that poem it would be hard to deny. Byron himself, in the person of Cain, is reasoning passionately, with unfettered brain, on life and death and divine responsibility. They are not original reasonings, they are old familiar eighteenth-century ones; yet the poet, with a freedom and fierceness like that of a sea-eagle, makes them his own. Still, there is hardly grandeur of expression. It is just in *Cain* that his sins of diction and metre swarm most abundantly. Continually, the eagle comes to earth, and walks, or hops, and is absurd. After Milton, you can hardly read *Cain*. Not that Byron is lacking in the sublime of a certain order. It comes in unexpected places, no doubt. Once again Goethe may be quoted. Talking to Crabb Robinson, as they read over the *Vision of Judgment* together, Goethe picked out certain stanzas for especial praise, and one, he said, was 'sublime'. At any rate it shows Byron's nearest approach to that quality, and it wins its effect and relief by being set between two purely satiric stanzas. The first of these, preceding the 'sublime' one, introduces George the Third arriving at Heaven-Gate:

> While thus they spake, the angelic caravan,
>     Arriving like a rush of mighty wind,
> Cleaving the fields of space, as doth the swan
>     Some silver stream (say Ganges, Nile, or Inde,
> Or Thames, or Tweed), and 'midst them an old man
>     With an old soul, and both extremely blind,
> Halted before the gate, and in his shroud
> Seated their fellow-traveller on a cloud.

Then comes Milton's arch-rebel:

> But bringing up the rear of this bright host
>     A Spirit of a different aspect waved
> His wings, like thunderclouds above some coast
>     Whose barren beach with frequent wrecks is paved;
> His brow was like the deep when tempest-toss'd;
>     Fierce and unfathomable thoughts engraved
> Eternal wrath on his immortal face,
> And *where* he gazed a gloom pervaded space.

It is certainly magnificent; and if Satan is here rather too like the familiar Byronic hero, it is just because that unsatisfactory personage, in his origins, goes back, through a mass of forgotten stories— the so-called 'fiction of terror'—to whom but to Milton's Satan?

## VI

But the *Vision of Judgment* suggests a last question, and a serious one, which takes us out of the confines of poetry, into the region where prose and poetry meet; and it is this: *What can Byron do to amuse us?* Amuse, that is either grimly or lightly, over the whole range, from high satire down to facetious high spirits? Nothing, we know, is so precarious, or wears out so easily, as the wit and satire of a given age. How much, in this line, of Shakespeare, of Swift, of Dickens, has become, to speak honestly, totally impossible to laugh at! I have a private belief that as humorists Fielding and Goldsmith stand almost undimmed; but let that pass. There is plenty in Byron that makes us echo the famed words of Queen Victoria when she was told a certain story. We have to pass over a good deal of mere horseplay, blunt farce, blunter innuendo, and what may be called a prolonged sniggering over the obvious. Byron is amused; we are not. He remained young after all, and on a certain side he never quite grew up. But then, we discount this fact, we know all about it, and all about Byron's streak of commonness, and no more need be said on that score. He remains, I think, when all is said, a true wit; and, using the term in its bolder not its finer sense, a true humorist. We should all agree that his general progress as a poet, leaving out his first essays, was from romance and declamation to satire and portraiture. Romance, indeed, remains to the last, and blends with satire into a most singular flashing web; but satire, after all, comes to rule. Now the principle of satire is reason, reason commenting mockingly upon absurd or base realities. Its natural medium is prose; but it falls into verse whenever the gaiety of the mocker sings itself into a tune and demands the cymbals, or when the wrath of the moralist demands a louder blast as an accompaniment. Byron, as we know, used both prose and verse. When he was young, it was thought that he would be an orator; he says himself that as a schoolboy 'my qualities were much more oratorical than poetical'; and oratory, we know, is own brother to satire and invective. There is wit, I think, even in Byron's youthful speeches in the House of Lords; when, for instance, he pleads for the removal of oppression from the Irish Catholics, and, pointing out that even the negroes had been set free, exclaims, 'I pity the Catholic peasantry for not having had the good fortune to be born black.' I do not dwell on the *English Bards*, of which he was afterwards ashamed, the satire having fallen wildly on many innocent heads. It is Pope, or Crabbe, blunted and coarsened. But it is worth noting that *Childe Harold* itself, but for the timid dissuasion of friends, might have been something of a medley of jest and earnest, like *Don Juan*. The suppressed stanzas have been saved; and there is the satire on the mock inquiry into the conduct of the generals after the Convention of Cintra:

Thus unto Heav'n appeal'd the people; Heaven,
Which loves the lieges of our gracious king,
Decreed, that ere our Generals were forgiven,
Inquiry should be held about the thing.
But Mercy cloak'd the babes beneath her wing;
And as they spar'd our foes, so spar'd we them;
(Where was the pity of our sires for Byng?)
Yet knaves, not idiots, should the law condemn;
Then live, ye gallant knights! and bless your judges' phlegm.

More of this ingredient would have lightened the tension of *Childe Harold*; but when Byron got to Venice, and had purged his bosom of his hectic tales and of some of his confessions, he found his real vein and his real form, or mould, and he commenced humorist. The true counterpart to *Don Juan* and *Beppo* is found in Byron's letters of the period. It seems to be admitted that his prose, which is chiefly found in his letters, will live; and it will live by its rich, rough, rapid, spontaneous humour, as well as by its manliness. He is perfectly natural and untrammelled in his pictures of his various Venetian establishments, and afterwards in the tale of his dealings with the Countess Guiccioli. There is little romance or sentiment in the matter; much more of a cool, careless intelligence and reckless humour. He becomes a positive, antisentimental Italian. Stendhal, an excellent witness, who met Byron, remarked upon his freedom from the childish vanity of 'turning a phrase'. 'He was exactly the reverse', says Stendhal, 'of an academician; his thoughts flowed with greater rapidity than his words, and were free from all affectation or studied grace.' And this, too, is the charm of his satires; you do not know, nor does he, what will come next; except that the jest will never be far off. It is very odd that amidst these brilliant achievements he went on writing his duller dramas, the *Sardanapaluses* and *Werners*, of which I need only say that he meant them as a tribute to the classic proprieties and unities, which in his naïve way he thought were still respectable. He sacrificed to the goddess of beauty, to the goddess of dullness, and to the muse of comedy, all at once.

VII

All three, no doubt, received their offering in *Don Juan*; dullness is not absent, especially in the more roughly jeering portions; much of it now reads cheap enough. But beauty, as I have said, is there; and comedy, or satire, prevails. Lord Beaconsfield, in 1875, pitching his words, as his fashion was, rather high, remarked that '*Don Juan* will remain, as it is now recognized, an unexampled picture of human nature, and the triumph of the English language'. Lord Beaconsfield, with his un-English mind, his vein of not wholly false romance, and his genius as a fellow-satirist, is another good witness. True, he could hardly have said more of Shakespeare's best comedies. But an *unexampled* picture, speaking literally, *Don Juan* is. Allow for all the blemishes, and there remains a surprising balance of wit, of observation, and also of a certain, not contemptible, kind of pathos. His hero is a peg for the adventures, which are mostly amorous; and as for the impropriety, I will for the last time quote Goethe, who said that 'poets and romancers, bad as they may be, have not yet learned to be more pernicious than the daily newspapers which lie on every table'. It may be added that the amorous scenes, though they do not satisfy and

66

clear the imagination like Marlowe's *Hero and Leander*, do not, for adult readers, either baulk and chill the imagination, or merely heat it. Juan, moreover, and even whilst he is in the thick of his amours, is made, very skilfully, to retain our regard. He is brave and humane, and there is no cruelty or 'bilking' in his composition; and, except in the bad episode, where he is a half-reluctant party, of his commerce with Catherine of Russia, he retains traces of honour. ('In royalty's vast arms he sigh'd for beauty.') Everywhere we come on that curious fundamental coolness and freedom of mind, and that dominance of reason, which emerges from Byron's torments, mysteries, posings, and from his more or less factitious confessions of wickedness and weakness. As a painter of manners, who has left a genuine 'document' behind him, his position seems to be safe. The Near East, and the London of the Regency—these are his two great hunting-grounds; and the latter cantos of *Don Juan* are a real addition to the memoirs of Regency England. Again we go back to the previous century for our comparisons. The true parallel to these scenes and persons, and to Byron's letters, is to be found not in the literature of romance at all, but in the letters and records of the serene, imperturbable old patrician free-living wits of the middle and later eighteenth century. Such are George Selwyn, and 'Gilly' Williams, and that fourth Duke of Queensberry who is not so bad as he has been painted. And Byron's strong, natural prose, as he pours out his stories and memories, is in essence *their* prose; it is not that of the age or set of Keats, and Leigh Hunt, and Wordsworth, and Shelley. It is penetrated throughout with a masculine humour, coarse no doubt in fibre, but not in the least feeble or insidious or precious. And the same tone, the same diction, reign in his verse, in the pliable octave measure, which wavers and changes with every mood and gust. Why, you hear the gay light old verse of the last age even in the *Hours of Idleness*:

> Why should you weep like Lydia Languish
> And fret with self-created anguish?
> Or doom the lover you have chosen
> On winter nights to sigh half frozen;
> In leafless shades to sue for pardon,
> Only because the scene's a garden?

I will add, that if we are asking what Byron can give us to-day, and to what gap in contemporary poetry his performance points, one reply will be, that we have had no new *Don Juan*. We have (1924) no great satirist in verse; the art seems to be lost. We have nobody with a large, free, gay, unflinching knowledge of the world, and with the ability to express that knowledge in verse. Allowing for the vast and obvious differences, Byron, at the opening of the nineteenth century, occupies a position not wholly unlike that of Swift at the opening of the eighteenth. Have we a Swift? We have, in prose, Bernard Shaw; but I will not dwell on the difference in power, or on Swift's deeper and sounder humanity. We certainly have had no Byron. In one sense, in the sense in which Flaubert said, 'Toutes les époques sont atroces'; every age is fodder for the satirist. In another sense, our own age seems especially vulnerable. But the paralysis of great literary art which has been caused by the world-convulsion, and which seems to have inhibited the largest kinds of poetry, has also left poetic satire comparatively mute. Moreover, if we look far back, do we find any English satire in rhyme that approaches *Don Juan*, if we reckon quality, variety, and mass all together? The *Dunciad* shows great power; but who except a student can read it for amusement? *Absalom and Achitophel* is a great and finished production, but it is only of the middle length.

I have said nothing of the Byron who went to Greece, who upheld the freedom of little nations, and who exclaimed that 'the peoples will conquer in the end'; or of his sufferings, or of their problematical causes. People will always make books about him, as they will about Hamlet; for it is the man that tells us most about himself, who remains the most mysterious. These are only stray notes on Byron's art and genius; they are an effort to intimate what he still can say to us when all mere enthusiasm, and all mere revulsion, have cleared themselves away.

# Robert Bridges and
## The Testament of Beauty

I have little right to speak of Dr. Bridges as a man; but, like many Oxonians, I had the honour of a friendly acquaintance with him during his last two years; and more than once found him, on his height above Oxford—whose towers are to be seen far below through his favourite rift in the trees— pacing on his lawn, cordial to the stranger, ready to question, and also ready to talk, not least about his own craft. He liked to discourse on the niceties of metre and on his own practice and experiments. I never heard him read, but believe that he did so in a style that matched with his presence, so noble and magnificently crowned. It must have pleased him that unprofessional persons, innocent of metrical theory, found they could read the *Testament of Beauty* aloud—up to a point—with little effort and merely by following the natural rhythm. But I leave these few, prized reminiscences; nor will I indulge in a technical discourse on prosody. The measure of the *Testament* already appears in Bridges' previous volumes of 1920 and 1925; it is there, he says, 'in the writer's latest manner, and still peculiar to himself'. It seems to grow out of Milton's usage in *Samson Agonistes*, especially his freer usage in the choruses; and the 'loose alexandrines' are based, we hear, 'on the secure bedrock of Milton's prosody'. Of this, as we know, Bridges had long before published his classic analysis. Only, of course, the base of the new measure is not ten syllables but twelve. It is used not only in the *Testament* but in the earlier *College Garden* and *Poor Poll*; as well as in *Come si quando*, where the high metaphysical style is already clearly developed. The exact formula of the verse, and the principles of its modulation, can be disputed; but one view is clearly set forth in Mr. Nowell Smith's valued book, for which we are all grateful, of *Notes* on the poem. A slightly different one is offered by an instructive reviewer in *The Times Literary Supplement* of 20 August, 1931. But to come to the subject-matter.

The term *Testament* signifies, first of all, the bequest and message of Beauty herself to the world; and also, that conception of Beauty which is the peculiar bequest of the poet. These two meanings, however, soon coalesce, all the more that the poem aims at, and often though not always attains, the realization of beauty, both outward and spiritual, in words; and I shall quote from the passages that do this most conspicuously, rather than from the harder and more rugged ones. Those, however, have their indispensable place, not only in the argument but in the poetic effect, like the philosophical or theological parts of Lucretius, of *Paradise Lost*, and of the *Prelude*. The critical question, it will appear, is when and how far these harder passages can be considered poetry; for there is no doubt about the others.

Beauty, as presented to the senses and the mind, is the natural theme of all poets, and also is, or should be, a main property of their form and expression. I say main, for it is not always the first word that we use; either, at one extreme, for the grandeur of *Samson Agonistes*, or, at the other, for such charm or elegance as belongs to a master, like Austin Dobson, of social verse. It is least of all natural to speak first of 'beauty', except in some transferred sense, when the effect, as in some great tragic speeches or impassioned lyrics, depends on discords, be they in the sound or in the sentiment. Still, beauty *is* a most frequent topic of poetry, and, when the work is good, is the most constant quality of its sound and language. As to the sensuous material, it is clearly, if considered objectively, the common ground and treasure of all poets and painters, and indeed of all men. Each artist dips into the same ocean of sights and sounds and odours, and holds up his scoopful in a different cup, of gold or crystal or commoner ware. The senses of each react in a different way, and the expression differs every time; still, they are all drawing upon the same world. But when they come to *think* about beauty, and of how it bears on happiness and behaviour, and of what is the relation of truth and goodness to the beauty of things seen and unseen, then they diverge indeed, and often seem to be speaking of different, even of contradictory, things. To Marlowe beauty is the face of Helen, or again the last touch, for ever unattainable by the artist. To Spenser, when it comes in human shape, it is no mixture of material hues and forms but the expression of a heavenly something which only intelligence, or rather intellectual vision, can apprehend. Shakespeare describes his friend as 'truth in beauty dyed'; to Keats, or perhaps to the spirit of the Grecian Urn (for this is a question debated), the two seem to be identical. Again, towards the end of the last century the very word fell into a certain disrepute; it became associated with a kind of cant, as if it were something only for the elect, not to be touched by the vulgar. The vulgar retorted on the 'æsthetic' view in their own way, with a rude but telling humour. All this is a thing of the past; but one virtue of Robert Bridges is to have redeemed the word both from the priggish handling of it, and from the derision that followed. For him it is simply one of the holy terms of the language, like goodness or faith; it had been too often profaned, for him to profane it.

II

Along with Spenser, he is the chief English poet who has girded himself to reason out the question, but he is far more thorough-going than Spenser, who does little but expound—it is true with wonderful ease and melody—a number of theories, Platonic and other, and often hardly congruous, that were in the air at the time. Bridges tries to show the place of Beauty in the whole economy of thought: how it is to figure in our religion; by what steps the highest conceptions of it have grown up; and at what points in the course of 'emergent evolution' (the term occurs in the poem) the sense of beauty has been markedly quickened in mankind. He thinks of a driving force that presses for ever upward through the atom, through the organism, and then through all human experience, sensuous, æsthetic, rational, and spiritual. In this process beauty becomes, ever more and more consciously, *valued*, as well as perceived and expressed. To the poet, at any rate, it is a central fact; it is, to begin with,

> our daily bread of pleasur; enough that thus I deem
> of Beauty among Goddes best gifts, and even above
> the pleasur of virtue accord it honour of men.

But this is only half the truth; in the end, beauty is a conception vital both to ethics and to theology.

The argument is difficult, the poem full of excursions and backwaters; but it moves, in general, forward from a vindication and welcome of the messages of sense to the interpretation of these by the soul and reason. The *Testament* is thus a full confession, with posterity for the legatee. It is also, at least in English, a new *species* of poem. It does not, save by implication and on the way, set out, like the *Prelude*, to relate 'the growth of a poet's mind'. The topic, as I said, is the historical growth of an idea, and the place of that idea in the final outlook of the writer. It is the last fruit of a life given to art—musical as well as poetic art —and to philosophic thought. Bridges lived just long enough to receive the salute of the English-reading world to his 'testament'. This, no doubt, it is too soon to judge in set form; we, or rather our heirs, must stand away from it after a lapse of time, in order to see so intricate a fabric in true perspective. Nor can I attempt any real summary of the argument, here and now. Let me simply try to note one or two of the successive meanings, in the poem, of the keyword beauty, and to disengage them from the mass of enveloping matter; and then to add a word upon the *Testament* as a work of art.

Two passages, one at the beginning and one near the close, explain the inception of the work. In the overture the poet finds himself, like Words-worth, remembering the sensations of childhood. Though he is near fourscore, they are keener to him than ever; *he* has not, like Wordsworth, to lament their loss:

'Twas late in my long journey, when I had clomb to where
the path was narrowing and the company few,
a glow of childlike wonder enthral'd me, as if my sense
had come to a new birth purified . . .

He is like a man upon a hill-top looking down on

the plain, now so far off, 'so by beauty estranged',
as to be no longer familiar.   To the old man—if,
indeed, he be Robert Bridges—much of his past
becomes as it were both some one else's and his
own, far off yet still distinct; and again, though
distinct, wrapt in a kind of glory and with the
harsh edges softened.   Bridges remembers one
great 'highday in June', when he had come on an
old flowery garden; and he could have lain there
'ever indolently undisturb'd', watching the flowers.

> waving in gay display their gold-heads to the sun,
> each telling of its own inconscient happiness,
> each type a faultless essence of God's will, such gems
> as magic master-minds in painting or music
> threw aside once for man's regard or disregard;
> things supreme in themselves, eternal, unnumber'd
> in the unexplored necessities of life and Love.

The other passage, describing the last moments of
a glorious evening, presents Beauty as the consoler:

> 'Twas at sunset that I, fleeing to hide my soul
> in refuge of beauty from a mortal distress,
> walk'd alone with the Muse in her garden of thought.

The mortal distress, it is understood, was the death
of the poet's daughter.   He discourses with his
dreams, that flit about him like bats; and one of
them, coming as it were within a dream, reveals
to him that

> Verily by Beauty it is that we come at WISDOM;
> yet not by Reason at Beauty.

The 'wisdom' is 'divine wisdom'; and much of the

poem has been concerned with the special, the radical problem: How adjust the claims of Reason, the discursive intelligence, itself a slow product of evolution and all but our highest faculty, with the claims of *æsthesis?* What are their respective parts in the ultimate vision of the highest truth? By *æsthesis* is meant the sense-perception which in course of time has acquired the feeling for, and conception of, the beautiful. The general answer is that Reason, fly as high as she will, must depend at last upon these boons of the sense; and that her function is not to supersede either them or the revelations to which they lead, but to make them clearer to us, and more spiritual, and to correct any aberrations. It has, in technical language, a regulative not a constitutive function.

### III

The historical stages of growth in the apprehension of beauty are, broadly speaking, four:

1. It is, in its fullness at any rate, a sense peculiar to man—his 'generic mark'. In the presence of nature, he and he alone can respond with *all* his senses: to the message of cloud and storm, of the music of birds and of Beethoven, and also—a point over which philosophers pass more lightly—even of odours. Of these, too, there are 'a thousand angelic species', each, like the jasmine, with its 'unique spice of perfumery'. So, too, with the pleasures of taste. In one curious and splendid

passage the poet seems to be carried away, and then
to return upon himself in a burst of moral satire.
His praise of wine is as magnificent, I judge, as
can be found anywhere in verse. To the eye wine
speaks like a jewel, to the nostrils like a flower,
to the mind like a rare violin, a Stradivarius of
perfect tone; in the fancy it breeds 'unfeatured
hopes and loves and dim desires'. Yes, but all
this is dramatic; it is the point of view, so we learn
(with some scepticism), not of the poet but of the
'voluptuary' who is making out his case: a futile
case, for, we suddenly hear,

> In such fine artistry of his putrefying pleasure
> he indulgeth richly his time until the sad day come
> when he retireth with stomach Emeritus
> to ruminate the best devour'd moments of life.

But this sally hardly interrupts the general celebra-
tion of the poetry of the senses, of the beauty that
strikes through all their channels. The ascetic
and mystic may scorn such things, yet he too may
be moved to do them honour. St. Francis, in
sickness and despond, made his hymn in praise of
all the elements, of 'my sister, Mother Earth' with
her fruits and flowers: a '*Bencitè* to be sung by his
bed'. This whole-hearted reception of the beauty
and pleasure that arrive through sense is, plainly
enough, anti-puritan; there is no rag of puritanism
about it. But, what is equally to be noted, it is no
less remote from the temper of the epicure, or of
the intellectual Cyrenaic who discovers the chief
good in single moments of pleasure, be that pleasure

physical or æsthetic. A version of *that* cult, as men of my generation know, gained in late Victorian times a passing and not too healthy vogue; partly, I think, through a misunderstanding of certain utterances of a great critic, Walter Pater. 'Simply for those moments' sake' became a kind of catchword. In any case, the beauty-worship of Bridges is totally different. With him, the emphasis is not upon the *ego* at all and on the satisfaction that it can squeeze out of experience; but upon the source and virtue to the *ego* of that experience; on the face of nature herself, and on the open-air life of man, and on history.

2. The second stage, or as the philosophers say 'moment', is seen in the process of *thinking* about, and of seeking to express, all these gifts of sense; and this the poet seeks to trace in the human record. For here, we find that both the sense of beauty and the desire to record it are manifested very late. Perhaps the poet forgets the lovely and now famous head of the Egyptian queen when he lays it down that the monuments of Egypt and Asia are 'wonderfine' rather than beautiful. He holds that it was in Greece, by the grace of Athena, that art first triumphed:

By such happy influence of their chosen goddess
the mind of Hellas blossom'd with a wondrous flow'r,
flaming in summer season, and in its autumn fall
ripening an everlasting fruit, that in dying
scatter'd its pregnant seeds into all the winds of heav'n:
nor ever again hath like bloom appear'd among men.

79

Yet, even here, one 'voice in Apollo's choir' was wanting to the 'full compass of song'. For the law is one of progress; new types, or dynasties, of beauty arise, though not without many blank periods and backslidings. The conception is not unlike that in Keats's *Hyperion*, a poem on which Bridges has left what is still the best piece of criticism. 'So on our heels a fresh perfection treads', says Keats's Oceanus in a key-passage. There is a reach, our poet thinks, even beyond the *Iliad*; nothing, however, has 'disthroned'

> bearded Homer's great epic of war;
> altho' thatt siege of Troy was in the beginning
> wrath and concupiscence, and in the end thereof
> tragedy was so tearful that no mind can approve,
> nor any gentle heart take comfort in the event.

Still, time and the Muse have made his story more beautiful than painful. And yet the 'philosophical concinnity of Greece' was not the last word. After many days came Romance, and therewith a deeper conception of Love, deepening that of Beauty. A splendid eulogy follows of the troubadours, who sang of the joys of life and resisted all chilling counter-forces, ecclesiastical or other. But the conception of Dante was profounder still, when he 'saw the face of a fair Florentine damsel as WISDOM UNCREATE', and 'lived thereafter in love', and embodied his idea in great poetry. The beauty of infancy and childhood, besides, was first disclosed by the Catholic painters; and the figure of Mary, *mater fons amoris*, sank into the mind of the West.

The whole of this argument leads up to what may be called

IV

3. The third stage, or 'moment', of the idea of beauty. It leads, that is, to the exaltation of love, in the form of Christian monogamy, as the ideal bond. The third book, on 'Breed'—a term that includes not only sex but all impulses rooted in the animal organism—is here our chief document. (I have, for clearness, not followed the difficult division and titles of the four books.) The love-lyrics of Bridges have long since taken their place in all memories and in the anthologies; now, in his latter years, with the keenness of memory which keeps him young, he watches love and reflects upon it:

> Beauty, the eternal Spouse of the Wisdom of God
> and Angel of his Presence thru' all creation,
> fashioning her new love-realm in the mind of man,
> attempteth every mortal child with influences
> of her divine supremacy . . . ev'n as in a plant
> when the sap mounteth secretly and its wintry stalk
> breaketh out in the prolific miracle of Spring.

The child prefers lovely things to imitate until his eyes are darkened by blundering teachers; and when he grows older,

> See then the boy in first encounter with beauty,
> his nativ wonder awaken'd by the motion of love;
> as when live air, breathing upon a smother'd fire,
> shooteth the smouldering core with tiny flames—so he
> kindleth at heart with eternal expectancies,
> and the dream within him looketh out at his eyes.

E.A.  81  F

4. There can be no cleaner view of the matter;
and it follows, naturally, that the whole antinomian
conception of 'free love' is foreign to this poet and
is dismissed by him as hardly worth his contempt.
In these matters he is in the conservative camp,
and we are not to look for any sympathy with, or
understanding of, the outlaw view. More and
more, as the poem goes on, closing with the book
entitled 'Ethic', the Christian terms become distinct: although, certainly, no special church or
accepted theology is commended: and, in the last,
or fourth, stage of all, the conception of Beauty,
like that of Reason, melts into that of Wisdom,
itself regarded as 'divine'. Wisdom now covers
the whole fruit of experience, sensuous, emotional,
æsthetic, intellectual, and religious. It is a pity
that the poem closes with a highly scholastic, if
exalted, summary of the writer's creed, where terms
like 'self and not-self' become identified, and all
differences are at last merged in 'one ETERNAL, in
the love of Beauty and in the selfhood of Love'.
A clearer key to the argument may be found in
another, now often quoted, passage:

> *What is Beauty? saith my sufferings then.*—I answer
> the lover and poet in my loose alexandrines:
> Beauty is the highest of all these occult influences,
> the quality of appearances that thru' the sense
> wakeneth spiritual emotion in the mind of man:
> And Art, as it createth new forms of beauty,
> awakeneth new ideas that advance the spirit
> in the life of Reason to the wisdom of God.

It is something like the faith of Prince Myshkin in Dostoevsky's story, that 'the world will be saved by beauty'.

v

Readers of the *Testament* will know that I have dropped out many a refinement in the text. Still, we can fairly trace these four main chapters in the story of the racial consciousness of beauty in its upward advance; and, to some extent, the individual is thought of as repeating the experience of the race. They are (to resume) first, the delighted perception and warranted acceptance of the beauty in nature; next, the double impulse to reflect upon it, and to render it in one or other art; next, or rather concurrently, the spiritualizing of the sense of beauty, in connexion with the highest sort of love; and lastly, the merging of all these phases, and also of the deliverance of Reason, in the vision of divine wisdom.

We are led to ask at once: From what point of view does the poet face the seamy side of the story: the general mystery of ugliness in the moral world; the evil of the misuse of the senses; and, in history, all the retarding elements of brutality, ignorance, and fanaticism? The simplest answer is that these things are not his main subject; he is showing the evolution of an idea which *has* after all sometimes triumphed, both in life and art, in spite of countless obstacles and of arrests that may at any time be repeated. But such an answer is too simple; and Bridges gives a new turn to the usual retort of the religious, that we are to acquiesce in a riddle which is beyond our reason. Do not, he says, ask *why* is anything; only ask *what* is; study the phenomena, in so far as they are revealed. Your reason itself is but a fraction of the universal mind, and the part cannot sit in judgement on the whole. We are here to examine what is knowable; and, in the poet's view, as his conclusion shows, we *can* truly know a great deal about our ideals, and about the mental destiny towards which we are called upon to work.

Moreover, as many a passage shows, Bridges is far from any sort of cheap or eye-shutting optimism. There is plenty of vehement satire, and much scornful reprobation of the ill things that hinder the progress of the soul. The passages on Sappho, and on the professors of Hedonism, will come to mind. Bridges, perhaps, is at his raciest and fiercest when he turns aside to denounce every sort of communism, socialism, and 'equalitarian' theory. He does not argue; he was not, I think, a man to argue with. But whatever their relevance, we owe some of the most splendid things in his poem to this opinion or prejudice. One is the picture of the bee-hive, which is presented, in its futile aimless round, as a type of a communistic society. Another, yet more elaborate, is suggested, we are told by Mr. Nowell Smith, 'by the recent finds of Dr. Woolley and his colleagues in Mesopotamia'; and,

as he aptly says, 'it is not clear what particular facts
of history are supposed to give the socialist a shock'.
The digger had found city under city, 'undremt of
in archeology'; and at last, a king's tomb full of
treasures, vases, seals, and instruments of music,
all ready for his use in the life beyond; and, amidst
the chariots and masks and silver heads of beasts,
'one rare master-work', namely 'thatt little native
donkey, his mascot on the pole'. But also there
lay beside him the skeletons of the grooms and
women of the harem who were sacrificed to attend
him on his journey.

VI

The conception of beauty set forth in this poem
does not fit very clearly into the long history of
philosophical speculation on the subject. We
hear little or nothing of the old questions whether
the æsthetic perception is defined by being dis-
interested, because it is free from personal desire;
or whether it is the one escape from the universal
'will to live', being purely contemplative and impersonal, and therefore never disappointed. This
last tenet, indeed, Bridges may be said to answer
indirectly; for desire and will, in his eyes, are not
evils from which we should try to escape, but forces
that are indispensable to the human spirit in its upward effort. Nor is he any man's disciple. True,
he often draws upon Plato, the fountain-head of
æsthetic theory; but it is more than once, to con-

tradict Plato. He will have none of the Ideas, which he calls an 'absurdity of indefinable forms'; and he insists that the two steeds, appetite and passion, in the chariot of the *Phaedrus* are not one of them evil and one good; both are good, or conditions of good, springing out of the, at first blind, impulse of life itself. The *Testament*, though it is less the fruit of methodic thought or reading than of a creed rooted in personal experience, is none the less, both for the moralist and the psychologist, a contribution to thought. I see that the lines 'Beauty is the highest of all these occult influences' form a kind of peroration to Mr. E. F. Carritt's valuable collection of texts, *Philosophies of Beauty from Socrates to Robert Bridges.* It is, as I said, a text not easy to connect with the rest of the story. As for beauty being the 'highest' of the influences in question; higher even than goodness which is a matter of ethics, and than truth, the object of science and philosophy—well, that is the natural creed of a poet and artist, to whom goodness and truth come charged at every point with the messages of beauty, and who, as we saw, finally absorbs them all in the conception—not in itself exactly a philosophical one—of Wisdom. When he exalts Beauty, in this sense, above everything else, we think, perhaps fancifully, of Milton's peculiar cast of trinitarian theology, and of the position held therein by the senior member. It would be vain, I think, to look in Bridges' poem for any such rigid background of system, such as Milton has furnished for his own.

*The Testament of Beauty*

Indeed, it is high time to touch on the *Testament
of Beauty* simply as a poem, and to ask—though
here again the answer must wait for time, and I
only throw out suggestions—how far it is a success.

Apart from theory and superstructure, its true
motto is found in some lines printed a few years
earlier, in the poem called *Tapestry*. Here Bridges
speaks of the world as

the decorated room wherein my spirit hath dwelt
from infancy a nursling of great Nature's beauty
which keepeth fresh my wonder as when I was a child.

For some forty years we had all known that his
muse was fostered in this fashion. His nature-
poems, chiefly lyrical, were his best-remembered
work; and they have found their place, along with
some of the elegies and odes, in all the treasuries.
His genius seemed to be lyrical, and also medita-
tive, rather than strictly speaking speculative. It
was often too delicate, and at first sight apparently
too *pale*, for the larger public, who ask above all
to be hit in the midriff. But the ignorant, when
they come upon perfect and studious finish, are
apt to impute such virtues to a want of passion.
We need not spend time on that imputation. But
this I think is true, that Bridges, a master of many
forms, had never, until he developed the style and
measure used in the *Testament*, found a form that

left him perfect freedom of expression: one that
would give voice to all the moods, passions, whims,
dreams, exaltations, prejudices, memories, of the
natural man.   His *Testament* is in the tone of talk;
it has more of the movement of talk, of talk falling
into tune, than we find even in his lyric; more,
certainly, than we find in his admirable, but comparatively orderly, blank verse.   Of the actual
metre, the 'loose alexandrines', I have said something already; and in the language itself, in its range
of pitch, there is no less variety.   The start is often,
deliberately, colloquial; and then the style rises, by
a slow succession of tones, to something like
grandeur.   We think, for instance, of the satiric
scene of the English garden-party ('Who hath not
known this pictur?—on a hot afternoon . . .'),
given by some 'vext politician', with its tables and
tennis-nets; and in the midst there is a classic statue
standing there 'in true ideal nakedness', gazing
on the idlers who 'blurt perchance A shamefast
shallow tribute to its beauteous presence'.   But
this is a long epic simile; and a simile for what?
For the true, ideal soldier, the Happy Warrior, as
he appears in the 'common concourse of men':

> mute witness and martyr of spiritual faith, a man
> ready at will to render his life to keep his soul.

There are many such descriptions that turn out
to be little allegories, ending in some sharp point.
Such are the pictures of the bee-community, or of
the Assyrian diggings, alluded to before; and these

come, as it were, midway between the passages of
pure poetry, on flowers and odours and sunsets and
landscapes, and those in the more abstract and
technical manner.   Of the former kind, praise is
needless; it has only to be said that there is a more
impetuous movement and a more crowded wealth
of colour than in the author's purely lyrical verse.
Only a poet who had already mastered classic form
and its discipline could thus afford to let himself
go and to spill his treasure without risk of confusion.

VIII

The difficulty of a philosophic poet, as we know,
is how to get over the stony ground.   We think
of the expository and theological parts of *Paradise
Lost*, or in Lucretius.   They are essential, they
contain the reason for the existence of the poem.
But if they are to be intelligible, they must do, in
great measure, the work of philosophic prose; and
yet they must remain poetry.   We may indeed say
that such prose, in the hands of Plato or Berkeley,
has itself much of the quality of poetry; and may
ask, Why should not the poet, in his turn, work
in the field of the philosopher?   But the fallacy is
plain; for the prose writer, like Berkeley, is for ever
moving *upwards*, in respect of his style, and may go
as high as he can; while the poet, when reasoning
on abstractions, is ever moving downwards, towards
the danger-point of the dry and scholastic.   Every

reader of Milton or the *De Rerum Natura* feels this check; and in the *Testament* the problem is the same. Dante, if any one, has solved it, in certain parts of the *Paradiso*, through a sheer mastery of form; one condition of which, doubtless, is the rigid precision of the system that is behind. For the same reason, many a discourse of Lucretius on atoms and the void gives a poetic pleasure. And they are wonderful oases—it is hard to say more —in the doctrinal speeches of Milton's God the Father. As to the *Testament*, a distinction may be suggested, which is useful also in reading Wordsworth's *Prelude*. It is simply this, that where the reasoning is rooted in some personal experience, and is so coloured and presented, it is more likely to be poetry than when it comes as bare impersonal argument. For this touch of nature, we can put up with a few technicalities and hard words. There is a sprinkling of them in the *Testament*, and doubtless they choke the verse. Only the loose alexandrines would admit terms like 'supersensuous sublimation', 'individuality', and 'euristic'. But they do not bulk large in the forty-three hundred and more lines of the poem. When all is said, Bridges has made a *new* style for English philosophic verse, and has often succeeded with it splendidly; more often, doubtless, on what may be called the high plateaux, than on the bleaker summits; and, in particular, in the ethical parts of the argument. Such is the finding of Reason upon the question of war:

## The Testament of Beauty

And of War she would say: it ranketh with those things
that are like unto virtue, but not virtue itself;
rather, in the conscience of spiritual beauty, a vice
that needeth expert horsemanship to curb . . .

The general style of the *Testament*, with its
naturalness as of talk, qualified by that continual
slight strangeness which lifts it into poetry; with
the freedom which the new measure allows and
indeed compels; and with its invariable, unstudied
nobility of accent, surely deserves all the honours.
It lends itself, for one thing, to long-drawn-out and
intricate harmonies, some of which it is not too
much to call Miltonic. I will end with one more
example, which carries our mind back again to the
old poet in his midland retreat, listening among his
trees on a spring morning. He is saying, once
more, that Reason has her strictly appointed place:

Nor without alliance of the animal senses
hath she any miracle: Lov'st thou in the blithe hour
of April dawns—nay marvelest thou not—to hear
the ravishing music that the small birdës make
in garden or woodland, rapturously heralding
the break of day; when the first lark on high hath warn'd
the vigilant robin already of the sun's approach,
and he on slender pipe calleth the nesting tribes
to awake and fill and thrill their myriad-warbling throats
praising life's God, untill the blisful revel grow
in wild profusion unfeign'd to such a hymn as man
hath never in temple or grove pour'd to the Lord of heav'n?

# *Alexander Pushkin*

## I

It is strange that so few of our classical scholars appear to interest themselves in Russian: 'a musical and prolific language,' as Gibbon said of Greek; with its flexible word-order, light expressive particles, and wealth of compounds. Its appeal, indeed, is of the widest, and the difficulty of gaining a reading, an enjoying knowledge of it—up to a point—is exaggerated. A friend of mine, a linguist, was too easily checked when he remarked that he was 'defeated by the elements, like Napoleon after Moscow'. That reading, enjoying, acquaintance is all that I can claim, apart from some lengthy ventures in translating Russian verse. The student of world affairs and the man of science, it is manifest, stand to gain immensely by possessing it. There is also a great and beautiful literature. The Russian novel is familiar in English versions; but the poetry is comparatively little known to us. The volatile essence of poetry, we know, must evaporate, most of it, in another tongue, and the translator must ever ask for much to be taken on trust; his hearers may sometimes wonder at his enthusiasm. Still, I am to-night offering some notes, with illustrations, on Pushkin, the acknowledged master-poet of Russia; who is also, be it added, a master of prose.

Alexander Sergyeevich Pushkin perished in a duel at the age of thirty-seven. The centenary of his death was celebrated last year by scholars and exiles in Britain, America, and Paris; and, on a mighty scale, by Soviet Russia. His works, it was said, were to be translated into some fifty languages within its borders; there were literary, theatrical, musical, pictorial, academic commemorations. One of his famed lyrics must have been quoted a thousand times; in which, following Horace, he promises immortality to his own verse. *Non omnis moriar,* he says, in Russian; the grass shall not grow over the path on which the people pace to his monument. 'In my cruel age, I glorified freedom and appealed for kindness to the fallen.' His name shall be known all over Great Russia and also to the Finn and the wild Tungus and the Kalmuck. Yet this is but one of Pushkin's myriad moods. Had he known, for instance, that his *Evgeny Onegin* was to be translated—for so I have read—by a wanderer at Telaviv into classical Hebrew, I am sure that he would have smiled. He does not take his fame too seriously. Elsewhere he writes:

> Meanwhile, my friends, drink deep, or rue it,
> Of this our life, so fragile;—yes,
> I am not greatly bounden to it,
> I know too well its nothingness;
> I shut my eyes to all illusion:

93

## Pushkin

And yet my heart is in confusion,
At times, with far-off hopes; and I
Should think it sad to quit and die
And leave no faintest mark in story.
I live, nor write, for praise, be sure;
Yet I would fain, it seems, secure
For my sad fate some share of glory.
One ringing word, befriending me,
Would keep my name in memory,
And stir the heartstrings of some stranger.
Perchance some stanza I have penned,
By fate or luck preserved from danger,
May into Lethe not descend.
Perchance, one day, some ignoramus,
—A flattering outlook!—at my famous
Portrait may point, and may declare,
'A *poet*—was that fellow there!'
So, take my thanks and gratulations,
Disciple of the peaceful Muse,
Thou who in memory dost choose
To keep my fugitive creations;
Whose hand, in pure goodwill, is led
To pat the old man's laurelled head!

II

I must not stray for more than a moment into
literary history; but let us remember that the true
renaissance, the first golden age of Russian poetry,
with Pushkin at the centre of it, is less than a
century and a half old; that it had indeed a history,
but no Shakespeare or Milton, behind it, and was
in the nature of a sudden flowering; and that it was
quickened, in great measure, by foreign influences,

chiefly French and English, which prepared the soil for the blossom. The tide of culture in the late eighteenth and early nineteenth centuries flowed from West to East over the northern Slavonic peoples, Russian, Polish, and Czech, in irregular waves and at varying dates; and in each case, after an imitative phase, the native genius was released and moulded; the Muse began to sing. Russia, in this renaissance, had one vast advantage, and a long start, over her neighbours. Her state was at least united. The Poles and Czechs were politically dismembered or repressed; it was their language, in each case, that kept the national soul alive through dispersion, martyrdom, and outward servitude. Poland produced a poet, Mickiewicz, the friend and compeer of Pushkin; he wrote his masterpiece in exile, in France. But in Tsarist Russia, despite all censorship and oppression, art and letters were *relatively* free. Pushkin, though sadly harried and much blue-pencilled, could be more outspoken in print—except in matters that touched the state or the faith—than the poets of Regency England.

I want to hasten to his verse, and can only touch upon his career. This can be studied at length in the new Life, so full and judicial, by Professor Simmons of Harvard; and there is still no better short interpretation, in English, of his genius, than Prince Mirsky's book, published twelve years ago in this country. The Pushkin literature, in Russian, is enormous, and still grows, and no foreigner could pretend to master it without years of study.

*Pushkin*

## III

Pushkin was born in Moscow in 1799; his family
is described as belonging to the 'middle noblesse'.
He had an Abyssinian great-grandfather, Hannibal,
a protégé of Peter the Great; and he liked to pro-
claim that his own blood was hot and African; also
to caricature the African signs in his features.
Pushkin's parents were neglectful, even unkind;
and his chief consoler during childhood was his
nurse Arina, whom he has made famous, and who
would talk him to sleep, and fill his dreams, with
Russian folk-stories. This kind of lore was to
inspire some of his most perfect poems. But the
culture of Pushkin's home and his second language
were French; a profound mark was left upon him
by French form and French discipline: by the
writers of the *grand siècle*, by Voltaire, with his
irreverence and wit and form; and by the martyr
André Chénier, with his feeling for beauty and for
the antique. Pushkin learnt the best lessons of the
'classical' age and quietly dropped its literary
superstitions. His contemporaries, Byron, Keats,
and Shelley, missed that discipline and had to
struggle towards adequate form without it. Pushkin, even in his boyish rhymes, has a sense of it.
Developing swiftly, and passing on to Byron,
Shakespeare, and Scott, he applies it gradually to
deeper and more difficult material. In a letter
written at the age of twenty-three he speaks of
'harmony, poetic precision, nobility of expres-

sion, and shapeliness'. If we add 'lucidity' and 'economy', we are beginning to describe Pushkin's plastic gift, though not the effortless variety of his style and music. All these qualities united constitute, in the true and widest sense of the term, a classic style; and as time passes, they are the qualities in poetry that one finds to wear longest.

The precocity of Pushkin's gift was speedily acknowledged. After leaving his Lycée—itself a forcing-house of talent—he ran wild in St. Petersburg, moving in high society and also amongst men of letters. His sexual code was that of his time and his surroundings. His experience, now and always, was a quarry for the lyric poet, the satirist, and the future novelist. His verse is a mirror of his inward and outward existence; but a magic mirror, in which the bare events and actual emotions are transformed by art, often out of knowledge. He records, as if with equal ease, his loves and friendships and antipathies, his blasphemies and aspirations and regrets, his jokes and pranks. He was dyed to what he worked in; and yet his most precious gift, perhaps, is that of artistic detachment. He found time to write a playful, riotous, and beautiful, though still immature folk-story, *Ruslan and Lyudmila*. Yet it was fortunate that some rash and generous political rhymes prompted Alexander I to pack him off, under a not always rigid supervision, to South Russia. Pushkin was away for six years, which were spent in the Caucasus, in the Crimea, in Odessa and other towns. Latterly, after yet another scrape, he was relegated to his mother's estate of Mikháylovskoe. He had not become orderly or respectable; he had plunged into many amours, and into some genuine passions; but his production, during these years, was magnificent. We come on a new and great constellation of lyrics, and also on many Byronic romances, such as *The Prisoner of the Caucasus* and *The Gypsies*, which by virtue of their finer and cleaner workmanship have long outlived their models, the *Laras* and *Corsairs*. The great novel in stanzas, *Evgeny Onegin*, begun during this period, owes a somewhat superficial debt to the greater Byron, the Byron of *Don Juan*.

Pushkin's life was changed by the abortive revolt of December, 1825, which involved and swept away many of his friends. The new Tsar, Nicholas I, saw that he was no conspirator but a genius. Nicholas spared him, summoned him to Moscow, charmed him, deluded him considerably, and left him at the mercy of a bullying, galling censor—and yet, after all, gave him his chance. Again Pushkin gambled, and had escapades. Once he bolted to the army of Caucasus without leave, saw some fighting, and was hauled back. But he was again splendidly creative. He had finished his Shakespearean tragedy *Boris Godunov*, and now completed *Onegin*: both of them known outside the Slavonic lands chiefly, and of course imperfectly, through notable operatic settings. Pushkin, who had now acquired a reading knowledge of English, also read Scott, Sterne, and some lesser writers. He produced his wonderful 'little dramas' in verse, including the *Stone Guest*; namely, the stone Commander of the original Spanish tale, whose deadly grip is on the hand of Don Juan. Pushkin's prose tales, such as the *Queen of Spades* and *The Snowstorm*, and his historical work on the Pugachev rebellion, would require a lecture to themselves. In 1831 he had married the beautiful young Natalya Goncharóva; and so came to anchor, though in a stormy roadstead. Natalya loved gaiety and dance and fun, had no intellectual interests, and was no companion to Pushkin; but she was true to him. His letters to her are not passionate, but they are affectionate, delightful and witty, and also full of not ill-tempered remonstrances; one of the commonest words in them is 'coquetry'. He could never manage money; he plunged into unsuccessful journalism; he was sore vexed by officials and censors. But not a ruffle, not a wrinkle of personal chagrin, disturbs the surface of his rhymed folk-tales, or *skazki*—perhaps his serenest work—or of his great *Bronze Horseman*. Years before the end, on hearing him read aloud from *Onegin*, Mickiewicz had exclaimed, in Virgil's Latin, as though to a new Marcellus: 'if the fates at all permit (*si qua fata sinant*) thou too shalt be a Shakespeare'. They did not permit. Some of the facts are still obscure, but jealousy, detraction, and the custom of the time and country, forced Pushkin into the fatal duel.

*Pushkin*

## IV

I confine myself here to his lyrics, to *Evgeny Onegin*, and to *The Bronze Horseman*. Pushkin is one of the great lyric poets, and his instrument is of the widest range. There are light joyous songs, as it were thrummed under a Spanish window; memorial poems of comradeship, or friendship, or elegy; public and heroic pieces like his ode on Napoleon; fighting; popular ballads; jibes, epigrams, arrows; and, not least, love-poems, often marked by a passionate logic of feeling. How much they are dramatized by the poet matters chiefly to his biographer; they are universalized by his art. Of these I give but one example, written when Pushkin was twenty-nine; it is called *Remembrances*. This genuinely poetical translation is by Professor R. M. Hewitt of Nottingham:

> When trade and traffic and all the noise of town
> Is dimmed, and on the streets and squares
> The filmy curtain of the night sinks down
> With sleep, the recompense of cares,
> To me the darkness brings nor sleep nor rest.
> A pageant of the torturing hours
> Drags its slow course, and, writhing in my breast,
> A fangèd snake my heart devours.
> My fears take form, and on the wearied brain
> Grief comes, in waves that overflow,
> And Memory turns a scroll to tell again
> A legend that too well I know.
> Reading the past with horror, shame, and dread,
> I tremble and I curse,
> But the repentant tears, the bitter tears I shed
> Will not wash out a single verse.

There are several of these poems of regret and inner conflict, and they always hit hard. But to turn awhile to Pushkin's pictures of natural things. These have no trace of mysticism, nor yet of that 'loading of every rift with ore' that was professed and practised by Keats. They are pure in line and distinct in hue, like a first-rate water-colour. The South and the Caucasus gave Pushkin his richest scenery; but he is most at home in Russia. The country is a refuge from the noise and taint of the cities. He shows us the 'striped cornlands', and the 'azure level of the lake', by which the poet strolls, reciting his own verses, and scaring the wild duck to the annoyance of the sportsman in the covert. Or winter is there, and its sadness infects the traveller driving:

> Through the eddying haze and shadows
>   Now the moon is making way
> And on melancholy meadows
>   Pours a melancholy ray.
> Down the wintry road and dreary
>   Flies the troika, swift, alone,
> And for ever tinks its weary
>   Tiny bell, in monotone . . .
> Ah, those snows and wastes, no lonely
>   Fire, or blackened hut, beguiles,
> But, in slow procession, only
>   Motley posts that mark the miles!

Or he prefers the autumn, which always kindles him to write and which is free, he says, from sultry heat and gnats and flies: Or, again,

## Pushkin

The radiance of spring is chasing
  The snows from the surrounding hills;
Snow to the flooded lees is racing
  Down through a hundred turbid rills.
Bright-smiling nature dreams, and meeting
The year's first morning, gives her greeting,
  And bluer now the heavens gleam;
  The woodlands, still transparent, seem
A down of greenery to be wearing.
  The bees wing from their waxen comb
  And levy from the meads bring home;
The drying dales new tints are wearing;
  The herds are loud; the nightingale
  Warbles, at dead of night, her tale.

Often nature is the setting for the mood of some
personage in a story. The girl, Tatyana, is visiting
the empty house of Onegin, now far away, who has
told her that he must not accept her avowal:

The evening skies are dark, and flowing
  Gently, the brooks; the beetles hum;
The rings of dancers home are going;
  Smoke, flame, across the river come
From fishers' fires; and Tanya yonder
Long in the open fields will wander
  Beneath the silver moonlight's beams,
  Buried for ever in her dreams.
Alone, and ever onward pacing,
  Now from a little knoll she sees
  A village and a clump of trees;
The master's house; a clear stream racing
  Below the garden. Here at last!
  Her heart beats heavily and fast.

V

The Russians are peculiarly rich in folklore and
folk-story, and Pushkin drank deep of these well-
springs. Arina, we learn, told him yet more tales
during his internment at Mikháylovskoe; and he
knew some of the collections made by scholars. In
1831, in pleasant rivalry with a friend, he began to
make his own rhymed folk-tales, or *skazki*. These
contain, not indeed fairies, but sea-warriors and
sea-princesses, witches, fish talking Russian, imps,
devils, and the Golden Cock afterwards famed in
opera. In the Prologue to his *Ruslan and Lyudmila*,
Pushkin describes some of this population:

> A chain hangs down with golden fetters
> From a green oak tree, in a bay,
> And on that chain a cat of letters
> Walks round for ever, night and day;
> Goes singing, as she rightward ambles;
> Turns leftward, and a tale relates.
> Strange things are there; the wood-sprite rambles;
> The water-maid in branches waits;
> And there, on paths unnoted, thickens
> The slot of beasts to man unknown;
> A cottage there, on legs of chickens,
> Unwindowed, doorless, stands alone.
> With visions wood and vale are teeming;
> And there, at dawn, the tide comes streaming
> On a deserted sandy verge,
> And thirty chosen champions splendid,
> By their sea-uncle still attended,
> In turn from the bright wave emerge.
> A prince is travelling by, and, sweeping
> Before them all, a warrior brave
> Away across the wood and wave;

There, served by a brown wolf and loyal,
In prison pines a lady royal.
   Beside the dame Yagà there stalks
   A pestle; as on feet, it walks.
Sick king Kashchèy on gold is gloating;
There, the true Russian scent is floating!
—And there sat I, and drank my mead,
   And saw the leafy oak, and sat there
   Down by the sea. The learned cat there
Told me her tales; and one, indeed,
   Comes back to mind; I now disclose it,
   And care not if the whole world knows it.

Some of Pushkin's lyrics introduce the water-nixie
and the house-spirit, which in so many countries
are part of the natural scenery, no stranger than the
fish or mice. Once the nixie lures a pious hermit
into the lake, on which next morning the children
see his beard floating. The Brownie or Robin
Goodfellow appears in a short poem, which (in the
original) reminds us of Herrick:

To thee, our peaceful ground invisibly defending,
   Here is my prayer, O Brownie kind and good:—
   Keep safe my hamlet, and my garden wild, and wood,
And all my cloistered household unpretending!

May never rainstorm hurt these fields with perilous cold;
   May no belated autumn hurricane assail them?
   But helpful, timely snowfall veil them
Above the moist, manuring mould!

By these ancestral shades stay secret sentinel,
   See thou intimidate the midnight robber spying;
   Guard from all ill unfriendly eyeing
The happy cottage where we dwell!

Patrol it watchfully about; thy love betoken
  To my small plot, and stream embankt that drowsy flows,
  And this sequestered kitchen-close
With ancient crumbling wicket-gate and fences broken!

—Love, too, the hillock's slope of green
  And meadows that I tread in idle rumination,
  The cool lime-shades, the maple's murmuring screen:—
These are the haunts of inspiration!


## VI

Beauty of scene, beauty of craftmanship Pushkin plainly enough commands; but with any national poet we must ask, sooner or later, Does he attain to grandeur, to what our ancestors called the sublime? To grandeur of conception, realized in the work? And if so, for how long does he attain to it? Size and staying power count in this matter. Poems that defy time and possess grandeur may indeed be short; I shall come to one presently, *The Bronze Horseman*, which is of middle length; and to one shorter still, of only a few lines. Yet the old Greek critic said truly that 'by a sort of natural impulse we admire not the small streams . . . but the Nile, the Danube, and the Rhine, and still more the Ocean'. Such streams are Lucretius' *On the Nature of Things*, and Goethe's *Faust*; poems, too, that have the resonance which comes from a great speculative background. Now it is a misfortune that Pushkin's long poem, his novel and confession in rhyme, *Evgeny Onegin*, though it has a greatness of its own, cannot in its nature aim at the quality which we are considering, and which we must be so jealous in discovering, because it is the greatest quality of all. But in his lyric *The Prophet* we can and must discover it. The poem may not have any symbolic sense, or express any deep conviction of his own, and it is unique in Pushkin's works; but he is now, for one inspired moment, kindled to transpose into song some lines in the sixth chapter of the Book of Isaiah. There, in the presence of the Lord, the six-winged seraph purges the lips of the Prophet with the live coal from the altar; and the Lord sends him forth among the people to bid them make their ears heavy and shut their eyes ('Lord, how long?'), 'until the land be desolate; and yet in it shall be a tenth, and it shall return'. Here are Pushkin's variations; I am glad to be allowed to quote them in Mr. Maurice Baring's noble English:

> With fainting soul athirst for Grace,
> I wandered in a desert place,
> And at the crossing of the ways
> I saw the sixfold Seraph blaze:
> He touched mine eyes with fingers light
> As sleep that cometh in the night:
> And like a frightened eagle's eyes,
> They opened wide with prophecies.
> He touched mine ears, and they were drowned
> With tumult and a roaring sound:
> I heard convulsion in the sky,
> And flights of angels' hosts on high,
> And beasts that move beneath the sea,
> And the sap creeping in the tree.

And bending to my mouth he wrung
From out of it my sinful tongue,
And all its lies and idle rust,
And 'twixt my lips a-perishing
A subtle serpent's forkèd sting
With right hand wet with blood he thrust
And with his sword my breast he cleft,
My quaking heart thereout he reft,
And in the yawning of my breast
A coal of living fire he pressed.
Then in the desert I lay dead,
And God called unto me and said:
'Arise, and let My voice be heard,
Charged with My Will go forth and span
The land and sea, and let My Word
Lay waste with fire the heart of man.'

No, Pushkin seldom writes in that strain; but he does not lack for *heroic* poetry. He can rise to the height of his argument when he speaks of Napoleon, or of Peter the Great. His long ode on the death of Napoleon surely ranks—and it is much to say—with those of Manzoni and of Shelley. I give two stanzas from the ringing translation of Sir Bernard Pares:

Russia, our queen of war, take heart!
    Again thine ancient rights proclaim!
Bright sun of Austerlitz, depart!
    Rise, our great Moscow, rise in flame!
Gone are the times of bitterness;
    Our tarnished honour still we save;
Russia, thy glorious Moscow bless;
    War! war! our pledge is in the grave.

And later:

Then all the world flamed up in wrath;
    Europe at last threw off her yoke;

And straight upon the tyrant's path
    The curse of all the nations broke.
The people's vengeful hand upraised
    The giant sees across his track,
And every wrong is now appraised,
    And every injury paid back.

Pushkin returns elsewhere to the theme, when his heroine Tatyana is travelling through Moscow:

There by its oaken grove surrounded,
Stands Peter's gloomy fort, in state
And pride; not long had glory crowned it.
All vainly must Napoleon wait,
Drunk with his latest, last successes,
Till kneeling Moscow on him presses
Her ancient Kremlin's keys!—Not so!
To him my Moscow would not go,
Head lowered, in capitulation.
No welcoming gift, festivity,
For that impatient hero she
Made ready, but a conflagration.
Thereafter, plunged in thought, He came
To watch the menace of that flame.

### VII

Pushkin was not quite twenty-four when he first set his hand to *Evgeny Onegin*. Its composition covered eight years, interrupted by many other achievements. It was published as a whole, as he finally passed it, after endless changes, in 1837, on the day of his death. It consists of 5,000 and odd short lines; and he said it was 'not a novel, but a novel in verse—a deucedly different thing'; and he speaks of its 'variegated stanzas'. There can be no

more remarkable rhymed novel of modern manners,
a species of which in England we have made little
and which may be commended to our young poets.
But that is a pale description. *Evgeny Onegin* is also
a *poem*, full of lovely scenery, of wit, of pathos, and
of personal but elusive confidences. It is also sym-
metrically plotted, with all the digressions kept in
scale; not a meandering piece like Byron's *Don Juan*,
which avowedly suggested it. A few passages which
may strike us as mawkish, or of which the allusions
have lost interest, are carried through by the handiwork, by the artist's unfailing clearness and precision.
I give a bare outline of the simple tale, with a few
stanzas in English, Pushkin's metre being preserved.

Onegin is a young *blasé* gentleman, fop, would-
be cynic, casual amorist, and rootless wanderer.
Despite gleams of compunction and good feeling
he is hard to like; but he is interesting, and, like the
great world of bucks and coquettes in which he
moves, he is portrayed with a skill that would have
delighted Pope. He goes down into the country to
administer a suddenly inherited estate, and begins
quite well. But he is soon bored; and boredom,
ennui, spleen, *skuka*, is his besetting demon. A
young enthusiast, Vladimir Lensky, full of German
sentiment and idealism, becomes his friend, through
the attraction of opposites; and he takes Onegin
to visit an old-world country family, the Larins.
Lensky is in love with the younger daughter, Olga,
who is of a happy and birdlike temper. The elder
sister, Tatyana or Tanya, is the heroine, and Push-

kin's greatest creation; the ancestress of many a
girl in the Russian novel. She has fed her innocent
soul on folklore, and also on the fashionable
romances. She loves Onegin at sight; and after
many struggles, and a dream that is filled with
horrors, she writes him a letter, one of the great
letters of fiction. Her confession of her love is
charged with a dignity that warns us of her latent
strength of nature. Onegin cannot respond.
Truthfully, decently, respectfully, but in a tone of
pedantry which Tatyana is never to forget, he
explains that he has lost the power to be happy and
that they would be miserable as man and wife; and
he advises her to be careful, for 'inexperience leads
to grief'. She says no word and is simply unhappy.
Soon comes the tragedy. Onegin in a spurt of
irritation does what we should call a petty caddish
thing. At the Larins' dance he flirts furiously with
Olga, to whom Lensky is now betrothed. This is
an insult, and provokes a challenge from Lensky.
Onegin, sobered, tries to turn the matter off; but
in vain, for the social code, in the person of an old
retired swashbuckler who brings the challenge,
seems to forbid. They shoot, and Lensky falls.

> He lay, he stirred not;—what strange reading,
> That peace and langour on his brow!
> The wound that still was steaming, bleeding,
> Pierced clean below the breast. Even now,
> A moment since, with inspiration
> That heart had throbbed, with animation
> Of hope, of love, of enmity.
> The blood seethed hot, the life beat high.

And now, just like a house deserted,
All dark and still it had become,
Had fallen for ever mute and dumb;
The shutters up, the windows dirtied
With spots of chalk.   No hostess there,
Her traces vanisht—God knows where!

Onegin, distracted and remorseful, now wanders
out of the story for some years.   Olga is soon consoled and marries a Lancer; and Tatyana, crushed
and left alone, watches her go, and roams the
country.   Her feet take her to Onegin's empty
house, where she is left by the housekeeper, study-
ing his belongings and his pencilled books.   She
muses, and begins to have an inkling of the kind of
man he was; and she cares less than ever what may
happen to her.   The family decide that she must
be married, and they go to Moscow to find her a
husband.   She wonders what fate has in store for
her, and takes leave of her countryside, as it proves
for ever:

Her converse she is still prolonging,
As with old friends about her thronging,
With each beloved holt and lea.
But summer fleets too rapidly,
And golden autumn is before us.
Pale Nature quakes, like some elect
Victim, magnificently decked.
The north winds breathe and howl in chorus
And chase the clouds—and next we see
Winter, in all his witchery.
He's here! he hangs, in snow-dust flying,
On every oaken bough and bole;

His billowy coverlet is lying
On every field, round every knoll.
See, with his feathery shroud invested,
Flush with its bank, the stream arrested!
The frost is sparkling; glad are we
At Father Winter's game and glee.
And only Tanya is repining;
The winter she is loth to greet,
And breathe the powdery frost and sleet,
Or with new snow, the bath-roof lining.
To wash her shoulder, breast and face.
For Tanya dreads the wintry ways.

Swiftly, distinctly, with a vivacity that reminds
us of Chaucer, Pushkin relates the noise and farewells, as the loaded cavalcade with its eighteen
horses sets out; the primitive roads, the arrival at
Moscow with its cupolas, the pageant of the streets,
the greeting of the old, infirm, distinguished aunt,
and the loneliness of Tanya at the Rout, where an
old general is seen observing her narrowly.

Time is now supposed to pass, and she is seen
again, at a great reception, the wife of a Prince N.,
an officer, not young, who had been wounded in
the wars. Pushkin has left to our imagination—
though we are not unprepared—the stages of the
great change in his heroine. She is now a lady of
mark, not exactly beautiful, but perfectly poised
and much deferred to, holding her own with the
reigning beauty of Moscow. And now drifts in the
travelled Onegin, to learn of her marriage from her
husband, who proves to be an old acquaintance of
his own. He is presented, is received with cool

civility—and falls violently in love with Tatyana;
writes her a vehement declaration, and gets no
answer; but one day surprises her in tears reading
his letter. The poem culminates in her parting
speech. She reminds him of the past, praises his
decency in having spared her of old; and yet

> your exhortation
> I heard submissive then and dumb;
> And now, today, my turn has come.

Does he now pursue her just because she is high in
the world, and because such a conquest would
bring credit to *him?* Why, she hates the life that
she is living:

> This pomp, which all in tinsel dresses
> The life that I abhor so much;
> My evenings, stylish house, successes
> In the world's eddy—what are such
> To me, Onegin? I'd surrender
> Gladly, this minute, all the splendour,
> Glitter and vapour, noise, parade
> Of frippery in masquerade,
> For our poor house, and garden by it
> Left wild, and bookshelf; for that place
> Where first I saw Onegin's face;
> Ay, for that burial-ground so quiet
> Where my poor nurse reposes now
> Beneath her cross and shadowing bough.

But she married to please her family; she had been
indifferent to her lot. She bids him go; she knows
that at heart he is a man of honour; and, for a last
word—

## Pushkin

> I love you—why sophisticate it?
> But am another's, pledged; and I
> To him stay constant, till I die.

There she leaves Onegin, planted, and she departs. A sound of spurs is heard, and in walks the worthy, friendly husband, all ignorant of the drama. There Pushkin, also, leaves Onegin, abruptly; with a valediction to his hero, his heroine, and his poem. We are left wondering whether Evgeny can bear out Tatyana's faith in him.

### VIII

Pushkin's most heroic and his profoundest poem is *The Bronze Horseman*. In 1824 the tidal Neva driven by a gale had flooded St. Petersburg, causing much destruction. Pushkin, down in the country, heard and read of this calamity and brooded on it; and, seven years later, printed a censored version of his poem. In its full form it runs to less than 400 short lines; and he had, for artistic reasons, cut it down severely. It is rapid in movement, and close packed; I must only summarize.—A century ago, Peter the Great, musing over the mud flats which were then tenanted only by Finnish fishermen, had resolved to build the 'vast shapely palaces' of his great city: and soon

> To that young capital is drooping
>   The crest of Moscow to the ground;
> A dowager in purple, stooping
>   Before an empress newly crowned.

*Pushkin*

The poet pays his honours to St. Petersburg:

> I love thee, city of soldiers, blowing
> Smoke from thy forts; thy booming gun;
> —A northern empress is bestowing
> Upon the royal house a son!
> Or when, another battle won,
> Proud Russia holds her celebration;
> Or when the Neva breaking free
> Her dark blue ice bears out to sea
> And scents the spring, in exultation.

Then comes the 'grievous history'. A poor little government clerk, another Evgeny, is kept awake by the noise of wind and rising waters; he muses on his prospects of a rise of pay, and on his love for a girl, Parasha. The flood rises; next morning it swoops down, and Alexander I, watching it sadly from his palace, is seen despatching help to the drowning people. Huts are shattered, coffins swim in the streets, bridges are swept away. Evgeny is marooned and takes refuge on the lions that stand by Peter's equestrian statue. When the water abates he takes a boat for Parasha's cottage; but only the landmarks remain, the inhabitants have vanished. His reason gives, he breaks into mad laughter; he roams the city, a derelict in tatters and derided; and at last he finds himself once more under the Image with the rearing horse;

> Ah, lord of doom
> And potentate, 'twas thus, appearing
> Above the void, and in thy hold
> A curb of iron, thou sat'st of old
> O'er Russia, on her haunches rearing!

115

And then Evgeny, the smallest of human beings whispers defiance to the Image, bids it look out, and beware of *him!* This to Peter, who is still the greatest man in the world, though he is dead! But behold, he is *not* dead; for the Emperor seems to turn and regard him; and the Image comes alive, and the horse and rider gallop after the flying Evgeny. The verses resound with the hoof-beats:

> And rushing through the empty square
> He hears behind him as it were
> Thunders that rattle in a chorus,
> A gallop ponderous, sonorous,
> That shakes the pavement. At full height,
> Illumined by the pale moonlight,
> With arm outflung, behind him riding,
> See, the bronze horseman comes, bestriding
> The charger, clanging in his flight!
> All night the madman flees; no matter
> Where he may wander at his will,
> Hard on his track with heavy clatter
> There the bronze horseman gallops still.

Evgeny, with his demented eyes and shabby cap, wanders about once more; and that is all, except that on a bare island, where civil servants picnic on Sundays, is found a frail hut, Parasha's hut, and in it nothing but the body of Evgeny.

> In the ground
> His poor cold body there they hurried,
> And left it to God's mercy, buried!

*The Bronze Horseman* has been much interpreted; but there is as little doctrine in it as in the *Ancient*

*Mariner*; it speaks simply to the imagination. It is Pushkin's great achievement, in a new sort of heroic poetry; and it is cut from the Northern granite.

I can hardly end better than with Pushkin's own valediction to *Evgeny Onegin*: a dedication to a fellow-poet, his praises of whom all apply, unconsciously, to himself; for there is much of him in these few lines:

> A friend's regard is what I care for,
>   Nor think the haughty world to please;
> And fain would I have offered, therefore,
>   Some pledges worthier than these
> Of thy fair soul, thy dreams prophetic
>   And sacred, to fruition brought,
> They clear and living vein poetic,
>   Simplicity, and lofty thought.
> Still, take these chapters as I sheave them,
>   So motley—and be over-kind;
>   Some simple, some exalted find;
> Half-sad, half-mirthful,—so receive them,
>   These pastimes of a careless mind,
> Of wakeful hours, light inspirations,
>   Of years unripe, of years that wane,
> Of cold, keen, reasoned observations,
>   And signals of a heart in pain.

# Chekhov

Anton Pavlovich Chekhov died young, at the age of forty-four, in 1904, thirteen years before the Revolution.  His life as a writer opens with the eighties; it covers the reign of Alexander III, the period of continuing repression and reaction, and also the first ten years, in appearance more hopful, of Nicholas II.  Much of his work reflects the disheartening aspects and temper of those times.  As a story-teller he is the chief figure in the interval between two generations.  He began just when Dostoevsky died, in 1881.  True, some two of Chekhov's elder contemporaries, Leskov and Garshin, were still in their prime; and another, his friend Korolenko, was long to outlive him.  Tolstoy, who did not die till 1910, was still great, productive, and dominant in his later phase.  For all this Chekhov, as a novelist, seems to be the truest representative of his time.  His younger associates, Kuprin, and above all Gorky, begin a new chapter in the art.  I will not venture to fill in this literary perspective.  It has been done, and done with authority, by our best guide, Prince Mirsky, in his

*Contemporary Russian Literature.* Prince Mirsky
shows us how Chekhov strikes a Russian critic with
a wide outlook. I will only try to show reason for
the attraction which he exerts upon ourselves, an
attraction which I believe will last; for this, in the
case of a foreign author, is the only real question for
all but professed students.

In his own country Chekhov is a classic, but the
classic of a pre-diluvian past with which the present
has broken; of an age far more remote in spirit
than the age depicted in the *Forsyte Saga* is to an
English youth to-day. In 1892 he remarked that
he had been translated into all languages—'except
foreign ones'; adding, however, that he had long ago
been translated into German, and that the Serbs and
Czechs were encouraging, also the French. In
England he was little known during his lifetime.
His own ideal of a translation, he says, is that it
should be 'something light and ethereal, like lace-
work'; he would surely have approved the versions
of Mrs. Constance Garnett. To her, above all, we
owe our acquaintance with his best plays and stories;
and we can also read in English, translated by
various hands, many of his best letters. These are
delightful; they are usually cheery, sometimes melancholy, explosive, ebullient, full of light jest, and
free-spoken; the reserve of the artist is not there and
is not wanted. Chekhov held it his duty as a writer
never to intrude upon the story; 'not to judge his
own characters, or what they say, but to be a dispassionate witness'. He claims for one of his plays

that he 'has accused nobody, and justified nobody'.
In his letters we read of his way of life, of the sports
and scenery that he loved, of his friends, of his
vehement practical activities, of his canons of art, of
his faith and his code of conduct. Chekhov is,
above all, unpretending, and he would have laughed
at the overdone, semi-mystical laudations of some
of his admirers, English and Russian.

II

Anton, the third in a family of six, was born in
1860 in Taganrog, the big commercial port on the
Sea of Azov. The grandfather had bought himself and his children out of serfdom twenty years
before the Emancipation. The father kept a
grocer's store; but the business went downhill. He
was a cultivated man, devoted to music, especially
to church music; the home was cheerful, though
strict and patriarchal, and is well depicted by Anton's
youngest brother and biographer, Mikhail. It was
also religious; and Anton became deeply familiar
with the services, the ritual, and the church hymns.
He was overfed with piety, and said that in their
childhood they had all felt like 'little convicts'; he
was to abandon all formal belief; but he can portray
the world of a monk or pilgrim and the soul of a
good ecclesiastic. 'Our talent', he says, 'comes from
the father's side; our heart and spirit come from the
mother's.' From the mother came also his open,
regular, harmonious, attractive features, so unlike

Chekhov

the tortured lines of Dostoevsky. The face, said
Korolenko, had a touch in it of 'the simple-souled
village lad'. His mother also inspired in him a
hatred of oppression, and a regard for all defenceless
things, birds and beasts. No novelist has shown a
nicer and a less sentimental insight into children.

When Anton was sixteen the household broke
up; the parents went to Moscow and found it hard
to live. The boy was left at school; and while there,
as at college afterwards, he gave lessons, like many
a Scot or American, in order to pay his way. Then
he went to Moscow, studied medicine, and in 1884
was qualified. For many years he practised, and
in his writings he uses his professional experience to
the utmost. He often owns his debt to his calling,
which trained the artist in scientific accuracy.
Medicine, he says, was his lawful wife, literature his
mistress. In this instance the two loves harmonized
unusually well. It might be added that Chekhov's
stepmother, not an unkind one, was journalism—
comic journalism. Before he could earn medical
fees he had to live by his pen. Deep down in him,
though in moods of depression overlaid, is the
humorist and mocker who keeps his own secret.
For some five years he tossed off hundreds of little
sketches for sheets that bore such titles as *The
Dragon-Fly*, or *Chips*. At first they are mere chips,
light vaudeville stuff; scores of them are of no
account. We are startled by stray flashes, and that
is all. Soon the flashes multiply, and within a few
years we recognize a master of the edged and

121

humorous anecdote. It had to be very brief, two or three pages. These conditions determined the scale of Chekhov's narrative art. The germ is the anecdote; out of this grows a short, then a less short, story. His longest tales are never longer than a short novel. Even these, he was to complain, were too long. *The Steppe*, he says, somewhat unjustly, is a string of separate pictures, not *one* picture 'in which all the details, like the stars in heaven, blend into a common whole'. He could make a beginning and an ending; but when he came to the middle, then, he says, 'I *champ*'. Most of his early works have no more middle than a wasp, and they never lack the sting. For some years comedy rules, or rather farce; but Chekhov's peculiar sombre presentment of life is soon to be discerned: the luminous grey texture, full of sparkles when it is held in the right light. This quality was evident by the year 1886, which was a critical one in Chekhov's artistic career.

### III

In that spring he was stirred—'struck', he says, 'as by lightning', by a letter that came from a novelist of old standing, Dmitri Vasilievich Grigorovich. Chekhov had already attracted notice; he had quitted the cheap press, and entered into relations with Alexey Sergeevich Suvorin, the editor of the chief daily, the *Novoe Vremya*. To Suvorin, who was to be his intimate friend for many years, a multitude of his letters are written. But no one yet had told

him that he was an artist, ahead of all his coevals.
He replies to Grigorovich in a strain of gratitude
and self-reproach.  He has been, he says, careless;
he has not respected his own gift; he has never
taken more than twenty-four hours to write a story.
Still, he adds,

I have always tried not to squander upon a tale the images
and pictures which were dear to me, and which, God knows
why, I have saved up and carefully stored away.

Thus encouraged, he went on producing, still upon
the smaller scale; eighty or ninety tales, including
some of his best, are the fruit of the next three
years.  He had always had a passion for the theatre;
and, besides sundry farces and vaudevilles, he wrote,
during this period, two plays; these are *The Wood
Demon* (afterwards re-written as *Uncle Vanya*) and
*Ivanov*.  By this time he had a serious public;
his life had many facets; he travelled to the Crimea;
he had delightful country quarters in a village of
the Ukraine; he was welcomed in Moscow by the
men of letters; his correspondence becomes profuse,
and cordial, and bitter and gay.  But I pass over
this chronicle, in order to linger upon Chekhov's
greatest personal adventure.

IV

Towards the end of 1889 his mood was depressed
and diffident; it is mirrored in *A Dreary Story*, in
*The Seizure*, and in *The Princess*; and his health
was irregular.  He had, some years before, begun

to spit blood; he was a consumptive; but he took little notice of his symptoms; and he had in fact, fourteen more years to live. He now went off at a tangent suddenly. From the first he had a warm place in his heart for the criminal in exile. One of his early anecdotes tells of a thief planted in Siberia who is dreaming at Eastertide of home and of the Russian spring. The local doctor is frigid to him, and refuses to ask him to a meal; but does ask another, a more important thief—more important because he has stolen *more* and on a grander scale. The smaller thief had stolen in order to supply a heartless spendthrift wife, who was left behind. But behold, she now appears in Siberia, under the wing—of whom but the larger thief? The husband, who can do nothing, in a fit of fury kills his land-lord's pet bird, is turned out of his lodging, and is last seen in the cold looking for a new one.

Now, in 1890, Chekhov picked up some books on Russian criminal law; and we see him fired with the disgust of the reformer who is justly ashamed of his country. To Suvorin he breaks out:

We have let millions of people rot in prison; have let them rot at random, without reflection, and barbarously. We have hunted people in fetters through the cold for tens of thousands of versts; have infected them with syphilis, have perverted them, have multiplied criminals; and we have put the blame for all this on the red-nosed prison superintendents. Now all educated Europe knows that the blame is not on the superintendents but on all of *us*. Yet we take no interest; it is no affair of *ours*.

Chekhov resolved to see for himself. He started alone, with no official blessing or credentials, on a trip of some 2,000 miles across Siberia, in vehicles and on river steamers, to visit the notorious convict settlement of Sakhalin (Saghalien). The journey out is told in his letters; his report is given in his book *Sakhalin Island*. This monograph is a sober and dreadful indictment. Its interest, no doubt, is largely historical and sociological; only stray extracts exist in English; it is, none the less, a real book and a revelation of the author. We are too apt to associate Chekhov's name with his helpless or baffled dramatis personæ, and it is refreshing to see him at work in real life.

It took him six weeks to cross Siberia, and he passed through alternate layers of hell and paradise. One paradise was on Lake Baykal; another, on the River Amur, where he passed through a lovely land, on the edge of China, far from officialdom. Before this he had made his way through mud, and flood, and cold, and dirt, and vermin. Once he had had to cross the great river Irtysh:

> The further shore is steep; the near one slopes; and it is gnawed away, slippery to look at, and repulsive; not a trace of vegetation. The turbid, white-crested water lashes it, and flings back angrily, as if disgusted at having to touch the ungainly slimy bank, on which, I should think, nothing could live but toads and the souls of murderers. The Irtysh does not clamour or roar; it seems as if, down at the bottom, it were hammering upon coffins.

Chekhov was well received in Sakhalin, and stayed

three months; he explored the whole inhabited part of the island, which was then entirely Russian soil. There were about 10,000 convicts of various grades. He had free access to all but the political prisoners. He visited, he tells us, every household, and made an elaborate census, on cards, of names, ages, occupations, creeds, marriages, and no-marriages. After doing a certain time in jail the male convict became a settler, planted out on the island; and then, after doing more time, he might be free to go back to the Siberian mainland. Chekhov describes the whole social economy; the handicrafts, the hunting and fishing, the diet; the punishments, the fates of the runaways, and, in his grimmest chapter, the position of women. The female convicts were not locked up, but distributed to the settlers for service and housekeeping; they were far outnumbered by the men. In one of the lighter passages Chekhov describes how the males, in their best clothes, assemble to inspect the newly landed criminals.

They are turned into the barrack of the women and left alone with them. For the first quarter of an hour the indispensable dues are paid to confusion and embarrassment. The 'bridegrooms' loaf round the plank beds, say nothing, and morosely eye the women, who sit hanging their heads. Each man makes his choice, without sour faces, and without smiling, quite gravely, in a 'human' fashion; paying attention to their plainness, to their advanced age, to their jail-bird aspect; he scrutinizes, and he wants to guess by their faces, which of them is a good housewife? Then one of them, young or elderly, 'seems to him the thing'; he sits down by her and starts a heart-to-heart talk. She asks, Has he a

samovar? How is his hut roofed, with planks or with
thatch? To this he answers that he has a samovar, also a
horse and a second-year calf; and his roof is planked. Only
when the housekeeping examination is over, when both of
them feel that the affair is settled, can she bring herself to
put the question: 'But you won't offend me?' The talk
comes to an end. The woman is enrolled to settler so-and-
so, in such and such a settlement; and the 'civil marriage'
is completed. The settler makes his way home with his
consort; and, as a finale, hires a cart, often with his last coin,
so that the mud may not splash their faces. At home, the
woman's first act is to get the samovar going; and the neighbours, watching the smoke, say enviously, that so-and-so
has got a wife already.

Chekhov appears to have seen everything in the
island except an execution. He saw men chained
to wheelbarrows; he heard a long story from a
murderer; he was present at an appalling flogging;
he reports a conversation with a boy of ten who did
not know his father's name, but only that the father
had been killed by the mother, who was now doing
time in Sakhalin and living with a man. Later,
Chekhov finds himself in a little graveyard, and his
musings, we may think, would have appealed to
Thomas Hardy:

There is no need for any one to remember all these people,
lying under little crosses: murderers, runaways, whose fetters
used to clatter. Maybe, somewhere on the Russian steppe,
some old wagoner, by the woodpile or in the forest, will
relate, for sheer weariness, how in their village there was
once a robber, so-and-so. The hearer, looking into the
darkness, will shiver, a night-bird will cry at the moment;
and that is all their funeral service.

*Chekhov*

He returned, again through paradise, by Ceylon and India; and on reaching home he tried, through friends, to interest the empress in the lot of the children in Sakhalin; of these, he said, he 'cherished no little hope'. It is not clear what came of his efforts, or of his book, which is stated to have perhaps influenced certain changes that were made in the convict régime. The years that followed were full of public well-doing. Chekhov was active in the work of famine relief. In 1892 he bought a small farm at Melikhovo, in the province of Moscow: he converted it into a beautiful place; and it became, also, a headquarters for action. The cholera threatened that region, but Chekhov worked successfully to avert it. He gave much medical advice. He had never been canny or economical, and once said that his money 'flowed away as quick as a perch that has bitten at the tail of a pike'. He founded a library in his native Taganrog. He could also set others to work. He built schools, built belfries; and received from the peasants the grateful token of the bread and salt. He held offices in the local administration. He threw himself into the work of the census, which brought him, as Mikhail Chekhov marks, closer to the life of the people, and made him 'a deeper and more serious writer'. His later fuller narratives, such as *Peasants* and *In the Ravine*, testify in their stern faithful way to these experiences.

128

V

After Sakhalin the stories became fewer; often
they are longer than of old, and darker in tint.
Chekhov is more preoccupied with the lot of humble
persons, and with social problems, about which his
characters discourse at length. Sometimes they
talk too long; the problems have now lost their
interest. Still the author, true to his principles,
takes no sides. He must not insinuate an opinion;
his task is simply to show how two Russians *would*
debate about God, or pessimism, or the future life,
or money matters, or the land. But there is no
doubt as to the direction of his sympathies. He
became, more definitely and openly, Liberal. During the Dreyfus business, he was wholly with Zola,
whose *J'accuse* he found like a 'breath of fresh
wind'; and he quarrelled sorely, for the time, with his
friend Suvorin, the temporizing editor of the *Novoe
Vremya*.

In the nineties Chekhov wandered a good deal in
the search for health. At last he had to leave his
beloved Melikhovo; in 1898, he was driven south;
and he finally settled, with his sister and his now
widowed mother, at Yalta in the Crimea. In that
region he bought a property; and his life under the
hot skies, and by the sea (which he once compares to
'blue vitriol') is mirrored in several stories, such as
the well-known small masterpiece, *The Lady with
the Dog*. He was much engrossed with the drama;
after various failures, Chekhov's reputation was

crowned by the success of *The Gull*, of *Three Sisters*, and of *The Cherry Orchard*.  In 1901 he married the actress Olga Leonardovna Knipper.  His wife continued in her profession, and the couple had often to live apart; but the marriage brought happiness to Chekhov, to judge from the multitude of his letters that have been published by his widow. They do him all honour, and show his gusty, gallant, and humorous spirit; but should love-letters be printed?  During these years he often saw the aged, the still all-overshadowing Tolstoy, who was ill, but who was to survive Chekhov by six years, and who, if with certain reserves, admired his work.  For a long time, says Chekhov, Tolstoy had influenced him deeply; but at last he broke away from the Tolstoyan code, and became disgusted with the ethics of *The Kreutzer Sonata*.  Still, he loved no man more; without Tolstoy, he exclaims, they would all be as sheep without a shepherd; and, while he is alive,

every kind of literary bad taste and commonness, everything that is insolent or lachrymose, will be remote and deep in shadow.

During his latter years Chekhov was surrounded by younger writers: among them were Bunin, the poet; Kuprin, the gifted writer of short stories; and Gorky, whose talent Chekhov saluted and who has left the best literary etching of his friend.  To read him, says Gorky,

is like a melancholy day of late autumn, when the air is clear, and sharply limned upon it are the bare trees, the close houses, the greyish men and women—all so strange, lonely, immovable, and powerless.

This is half the truth; it expresses one of the moods that Chekhov's writings induce. In 1904, still hopeful and full of plans, he went to the Black Forest to recruit, and died at Badenweiler. He was buried in Moscow beside his father.

## VI

From first to last, Chekhov is a humorist; humour strikes across his gloomiest plays and stories like a line of sparkles on a tarn. In his early anecdotes it is rampant satire. His favourite victims are the official and professional classes, incompetent, servile, and absurd. We are still in the world of the rigid hierarchies originally designed by Peter the Great. Drink, too, is everywhere in Chekhov's pages, reeking,—drink on its ludicrous, or on its fatal side. Two advocates, 'in a superior frame of mind', blunder homewards, but into the wrong garden, and are entangled with the poultry in the darkness. A sanitary commission on circuit is detained by good cheer, and never gets to work. A coroner and a doctor driving to an inquest are diverted by weather, by hospitality, and by an amorous adventure which comes to nothing; they never reach the body. A defending counsel, day-dreaming about his children and also about a gipsy girl, drowses in the court and forgets his brief; suddenly he wakes, and sees that very girl in the witness-box. Or certain judges, in their private room, refuse to do business and talk only about eatables. In other legal scenes the point is the comic blank unintelligence of the prisoner. In *The Malefactor*, a peasant is being tried for unscrewing a nut upon the railway line. His defence is that he wanted a nut, and nothing else, for fishing, as a weight; for a nut is hollow, and it is heavy; and a nail is not hollow, and would have cost money. The court points out that he might have derailed a train and killed people. He only grasps the word 'kill':

The Lord forbid, Excellency! Why should I kill? Am I not baptized? Am I a bad lot? Thank the Lord, I have lived all my life and have not only never killed but never had such an idea in my head.

He is led away, still babbling. This tale was based on fact.

One of the best-known of these anecdotes is *The Chameleon*. The chameleon is a police inspector on his round. In the square he comes upon a small tradesman, who is pointing a bleeding finger and holding on to the hind legs of a dog. The inspector, indignant, says that the beast must be killed, and that he will teach people to let their dogs run about loose. But—whose dog is it? Some one says that it is the General's. The chameleon changes at once; tells the bitten one that he is lying, and that he had really torn his finger on a nail. Then it seems that the General has no such dog; and the chameleon is again sympathetic with the victim.

But is it, perhaps, *Mrs.* General's dog? Her cook says, 'No.' 'Kill it!' says the inspector. 'Ah,' says the cook, 'but it *is* the dog of Mrs. General's brother, who has just arrived.' The chameleon makes a last quick-change. 'Doggy', he says, 'is all right: so lively! the naughty thing is angry'; and he turns on the wretched tradesman: 'Thou shalt hear from me presently!' and the crowd laugh.

We seldom ask a lettered Englishman whether he has heard that really good story about a Mr. Bumble or a Mr. Squeers. Chekhov's humorous yarns are no doubt equally familiar to a lettered Russian. But I take my chance of their being strange to some of my hearers, and will retail one more. This is called *The Anna on the Neck.* It is of later date (1895); it is an interlude, amidst a series of longer, weightier narratives (*Three Years, My Life, The House with the Mezzanine*), and the old gaiety is renewed, but with a difference. The 'Anna' is the name of a decoration; it is also the name of the young wife in the story. She has been married, for the benefit of her indigent family; married to a rich elderly official. He is mean and pedantic. His wife's father is a tippler; and to this old man he doles out, along with a small loan, a heavy lecture on his habits. Anna gets no money from her husband; only rings and brooches, which, he remarks, are good things to keep against a rainy day. Anna's instinct is to live, to enjoy, to spend, and to spread her wings. She is sorely 'hadden doun'; but as they travel, on the dismal wedding-

133

day, she has one moment of pleasure. At a wayside station she comes by chance on a crowd of cheerful young friends who wish her joy. This incident we remember afterwards to have been a good omen. At last her husband is forced to take her to an official ball, and also to give her a proper dress. To his amazement, as he stands about and nips brandy, Anna is at once the queen of the evening. She dances and flirts with the officers, and with a young gallant, who had been one of the party at the railway station. Above all, she is noticed by His Excellency, at the request of his wife, and triumphs at the charity bazaar. 'For the first time in her life she felt she was rich and free.' But Anna is no mere butterfly; and there is the true thrill of comedy in the three words that she flings, on the next day, at her husband: 'Blockhead, get out!' The tables are turned; she now spends what she likes and goes where she likes. The official world, his only world, is now against the husband. Yet he has his long-coveted reward, the ribbon and medal of the Anna of the second class; and His Excellency vents his time-honoured joke: 'Now you have three Annas, two on your neck, and one in your buttonhole.' Anna is last seen driving with her gallant. Her old father, jubilant, tries to call out to her something cheerful, in the street, while his young children take his arm, and entreat him: 'Daddy, you mustn't! Daddy, that will do!' Chekhov likes, at the finish, to throw in a bitter word that carries the imagination forward.

He could write a tale for children; there is a delightful one, done in pen and ink with comic drawings, and reproduced in his correspondence. But, in his books, the children's tales are not tales for children. Now and then he is tragic, I will not say theatric; a desperate young boy shoots himself; a child-nurse, also desperate, kills an infant. In contrast, there is the merry picture of the loto party. Four small creatures, all under ten, are playing late at night for farthings while the parents are out; we listen to their chatter, and each of them is distinct. One cares only for the coin, another only for the game, another for neither; and the youngest, 'a regular little animal', only cares to watch for the quarrels of the rest. The cook's son joins in. They are last seen asleep, tumbled together upon a bed. It is a picture by an Old Master; Chekhov was then twenty-six.

Of the same date is *A Trifle from Life*, which illustrates well enough Chekhov's chosen method of winding into his subject. He likes to begin, in his own words, with 'life level, smooth, and ordinary, just as it actually is'. We are mildly interested; and some hints are dropped, which we do not notice until later. Then, at some point, there is a slight sudden swerve,[n] a *clinamen*, from the straight course, and the suspense is awakened. Then, at or near the close, a sudden phrase is heard, which drives in the point like a syringe. A youngish man, one Belyaev, ruddy, well-fed, and callous, is paying a chance call upon a mistress, a married lady, of whom he has long been weary; the husband has disappeared. Belyaev finds the eight-year-old Alyosha, the lawful son, skylarking about alone. They chat; Alyosha plays with the visitor's watch-chain, and is at last led to tell him, after exacting a promise of secrecy, something that mother must never know: namely how he, Alyosha, and his small sister, are regularly taken by nurse to a pastrycook's; and how there they meet—whom but the vanished father? We hear how father feeds them with pies, tells them to respect and obey mother, and laments that she has been ruined by Mr. Belyaev; and how Alyosha had told father that Mr. Belyaev was quite kind, and never shouted at mother. At this Belyaev is furious; his heavy vanity is inflamed; and, when the lady enters, he rates her viciously and charges her, wrongfully, and in spite of Alyosha's desperate signs and noises, with being privy to the business. She goes out in indignation. Alyosha, shaking and crying, exclaims 'But you gave your word of honour!' 'Get away,' says the fellow: 'this matters more than any words of honour!' Here, and not in the injury to the lady, is the tragic moment. Alyosha, says the author (speaking for once in person),

for the first time in his life was brutally up against a lie, face to face. He had not known before that in this world, besides sweet pears, pies, and costly watches, there are many other things for which there is no name in the language of children.

The tale of innocence, in fact, becomes a tale of experience; and Alyosha finds, in the words of the poet Blake, that 'Cruelty has a human heart, and Jealousy a human face'.

VIII

It may not be out of place to quote at this point some sentences from Chekhov's letters that set forth his own code of behaviour. They are found at wide intervals of date. In his youth, writing to a brother, he describes what he calls 'educated people'. They respect, he says, human personality, and their own talent; they are sympathetic, and that not merely with cats and beggars; they fear lying like fire; they abhor smells and dirt; they control their sexual impulses; and they work incessantly. Elsewhere he states that his own morality is very ordinary; he has failings in the matter of eating, drinking, and dissipation; and yet he is quits; for these sins have been paid for by their consequences. But he has not broken the Christian rule; he has not lied, coveted, flattered, or pretended. The result is neither plus nor minus; he is just an ordinary person. In another letter Chekhov sets up a much less negative ideal; it is, indeed, a confession of the faith which lies behind all his art:

My holy of holies is this: the human body; health; intellect, talent, inspiration; love; and the most absolute freedom —freedom from lies and violence. ... Such is the programme I would keep to, if I were a great artist.

137

This, we may agree, is a good working creed, on what are called naturalistic lines. More than once Chekhov disclaims any dogmatic belief. His mind was not, like Tolstoy's, doctrinal. No one has a sharper sense that all things are mysterious, than the born agnostic; and Chekhov liked to say, 'You will never *understand* anything in this world.' Intellectually, he came to cherish a faith in some very far-off time when reason and science and goodwill and decency would surely prevail. I will try to indicate, when I refer to his plays, how this faith becomes charged with feeling and expressed with many a beautiful, as it were musical, *nuance*. Meantime, in his stories, he discloses a rare dramatic and human sympathy with certain kinds of religious sentiment. Two examples may be mentioned: *The Bishop*, written in his last years; and the *Student*, written when he was thirty-four. The old, wakeful, dying bishop, who has risen from the people, remembers his whole innocent life and its vexations. One of his troubles had been that every one insisted on treating him as a man of God, as a man of rank; no one would talk to him simply as a human being. On Palm Sunday he goes wearily through the long service for the last time. In the congregation he sees an old woman who reminds him of his mother; and his mother she proves to be. A simple creature, she is embarrassed when they meet; she is divided between the thought of her boy and awe in presence of the bishop. He dies and is forgotten; she goes home, and when she ventures to say that she had once had a son in the hierarchy, she is scarcely believed.

In the other tale a young divinity student is returning home on Good Friday to his native village. He is in a weary mood. He reflects that in the time of John the Terrible there had been just the same freezing wind, just the same poverty, ignorance, and sense of oppression; and so it always would be. He then visits an old village acquaintance, who had once been a nurse, and her stolid peasant daughter; and suddenly he tells them, hardly at all in Church Slavonic, but in simple Russian, the story of the Apostle Peter's denials, and how Peter went out and wept bitterly. The women look at him, are moved, and burst into tears. The student goes away and reflects. Why did they cry? Not because he had told the story in a touching manner. The reason must be that the incident has some relation to them, and to himself. Then he seemed to see an unbroken chain of events stretching from that day to this. He had touched one end, and the other end had vibrated. Truth and beauty had guided mankind in the court of the high priest, and so they did to-day. Then a sense of youth and happiness came back to him, and life seemed full of high significance. Chekhov ends there, and draws no conclusions.

*Chekhov*

IX

But I have left out the setting of this story, the landscape; and without his landscapes Chekhov is not to be understood:

The thrushes were loud; and close by, in the marshes, some living creature was droning a lamentable note, as though blowing into an empty bottle. One woodcock lingered still, and the sound of a shot rattled gaily after him in the spring air. But when darkness had fallen on the wood, an unseasonable blast of cold piercing wind came from the east, and all was silent. Needles of ice lingered in the pools, and the wood became comfortless, deserted, and un-inhabited. There was still a smack of winter.

This chastity in natural description, such as we find in our own Thomas Hardy, seems to be the birth-right not only of the greater Russian novelists, of Turgenev with his unequalled music, and also of Tolstoy, but of writers less ambitious. The pictures of river and forest, of ice and snow, by Korolenko, are exquisite and deserve translation. Chekhov keeps, perhaps more strictly than the rest, to his canon that all such descriptions should be brief, should eschew routine (do not talk, he says of 'silvered poplars'!), and should exist simply to quicken in the reader a mood in accord with the story; let him be able to see the scene, when he shuts his eyes! Chekhov was himself an open-air man. One summer he is in a country house, near a 'broad, deep, islanded stream', one bank steep and high and overgrown with oak and willow; boats on the water; the sound of frogs: and

In the reeds some mysterious bird is crying like a cow shut in a stable, or like a trumpet to waken the dead, day and night.

In the stories, nature seldom rejoices; or, if she does, it is often as a foil to the cruel formidable village life, such as is depicted in *Peasants*; or, at best, as a momentary solace to the eyes of the pauper woman who has been driven from the village. In *The Witch*, a whirling tempest of snow imprisons in their hut the sinister sexton and his wife, and intensifies their discord. The best of Chekhov's landscapes, like those of the exquisite poet Fet, are in twilight; one of them I will quote, in order to introduce another, and a profoundly characteristic, type of subject. The teller, in the story (an early one) entitled *Verochka*, is recalling an episode of his long past youth; and this is how it had finished:

He paced back quickly to the garden. In the garden, and on the path, the mist had gone; and the clear moon looked down from heaven, as if it had been washed; the east was just overcast with fog. Ognev remembers his cautious steps, the dark windows, the heavy scent of heliotrope and mignonette. The familiar Karo wagged his tail amicably and sniffed at Ognev's hand. . . . This was the only living creature that saw how he twice circled the house, stopped at Vera's dark window, waved his hand, sighed, and left the garden.

The youth, who was of a bookish, rather timid temper, had taken leave, perhaps for the last time, of a cordial friendly family, after a long stay. It will soon be, so he muses, only a memory, like that of a flight of cranes over the sky. He had had no thought of love-making. But we are told, slowly, and with every shade of delicacy, for the theme is difficult, how the young daughter of the house had walked with him to the wood to see him off; how at last, desperately brave, she let him know that she loved him; how the youth, astounded, could only answer haltingly, and she ran back in shame; and how he followed her later, to look once more at the blind house; and how, for this is the root of the matter, he became aware of what he had lost 'through impotence of soul and incapacity for the deep acceptance of beauty'.

All the time, something had whispered to him that what he was now seeing and hearing was, from the point of view of nature and personal happiness, more serious than any kind of books and statistics.

But he had sighed, retraced his steps as described, and then gone away for good.


X

I have been dipping, all the time, in a lucky bag in which almost everything is a prize. There are many stories by Chekhov in which the ruling conception is some kind of fatal error, or *impasse*, or spiritual deadlock: a conception that has been made familiar by his plays. Anywhere, there may be a spirit in prison: in a villa, a hut, a hospital, a factory, a monastery, the edge of a forest; or, most impas-

sable jail of all, upon the open steppe. The walls
may be poverty, or distance, or solitude; or the iron
social scheme and the hardness of surrounding
persons. Above all, they are raised by the want of
wit, or of sufficient will, to push away and escape.
There is only the *wish* to escape, and the ineffectual
vision of some window, or outlet, which is too high
to reach. The result, in point of art, is that the
story has no definite issue or solution; and with such
a story the healthy Briton is apt to be impatient.
He fingers his moral muscles, and he says, 'Why
don't they *do* something? How Russian! This is
not a story at all.' Well, you have only to live a
short time and look around you, to see that an
*impasse* in life is not a specifically Russian thing.
And certain also of our own writers have shown that
it is not: Thomas Hardy and George Gissing and
George Eliot. Lydgate, in *Middlemarch*, the country
doctor with his spoiled ambitions and his crampfish
of a wife, is a thoroughly Chekhovian figure. What
is really Russian about the business is the peculiar
artistic method, which our novelists have hardly
carried so far, and its power of suggestion. It
comes out clearly enough in the elaborate study
called *My Life*; and this I choose out of many such
studies, partly to prevent any bewilderment, but
also because, like Chekhov's later dramas, it does
not end quite blankly. In some cases it is hard to
acquit him of being over-clinical; of feeling, and of
giving, the pleasure less of a work of art than of a
perfect surgical operation. The alienist in *Ward*

*No.* 6, who in the end joins his own patients, and the old professor, in *A Dreary Story*, who finds that his powers are failing and that his only friend has become strange—these, for all their power, I would call clinical studies. It is otherwise in *My Life*.

Here the speaker is a young enthusiast of noble rank, who is moved to 'simplify' himself, to quit the bonds of his class, to become one of the people, and to work with his hands: he is a real historic type, which has a special name, *narodnik*. He is duly denounced by his father and bewailed by his sister. He becomes a house-painter; he is cut by his friends, and at first is treated with hardship and derision by his fellow-workmen. Then comes a gleam of hope. A brilliant girl, an actress, who has no social prejudices, falls in love with him, or with his ideas, and marries him—for a time. Some money is saved; they set up in the country, try to help the peasants, to build a model school; and they fail. The wife wearies and goes back to the stage. The man carries on work with his sister, who has now escaped from home; she too has been through the fire; she dies, leaving an illegitimate child. The man remains a foreman, by this time quite well regarded. Now and then he meets another woman, who has loved him; but they never come together. They are last seen walking to the sister's grave with the child. The bright spot is the child—the eternal question-mark; and we remember Chekhov's hopes for Sakhalin. So the tale ends, with the characteristic no-solution, and yet less hopelessly than usual.

Who will say that this is not like life, not good and penetrative art?

XI

But how present a situation of this kind in a drama? The theatre seems to demand that something should really happen. I have left too little time for Chekhov's plays and will only touch on one feature of them, which partially answers this question. Acted in Russian, they have triumphed in London and abroad; the principal ones are also played in English. Even if never acted again, I think they must live as dramatic literature. I say nothing of Chekhov's excellent merry farces, *The Bear*, *The Proposal*, and the rest; he refused to take superior views and never lost his relish for simple fun. To his four serious pieces, *The Gull*, *Uncle Vanya*, *The Three Sisters*, and *The Cherry Orchard*, should be joined one more, the early *Ivanov*. There was a pre-ordained harmony between Chekhov's talent and that of the Russian Artistic Theatre, which made and saved his fame as a playwright; and a corresponding harmony, it appears, among the players themselves, none of them usurping the scene, and all of them, like an orchestra, subserving the effect. This, indeed, is in several cases a violent one; in *The Gull*, for instance, the climax is a suicide. But such an ending is no less foreign to Chekhov's proper craft than is the 'happy ending' which for centuries was part of the very definition of a comedy.

His true achievement, and that of the players, was to carry across to the audience his peculiar strain of poetic musing and his picture of an action in which, externally, nothing is accomplished. To do this, to supply the want with some idea to which the imagination can return and fix itself, Chekhov came to employ an instrument which it is terribly easy to jar and even to make ridiculous. This is the symbol; or, to use a less abstract word, the burden or refrain. Sometimes, as in *The Gull*—and as in Ibsen's *Wild Duck*—the symbol is definite; it is in the centre of the stage. The shot bird is there; it is seen, and is at once appropriated to herself, by the chief sufferer. This is the stage-struck girl, Nina, who has been blandished by the second-rate cele-brated author Trigorin, and misled into the wrong profession. She becomes an actress and finds she is a poor one. But the symbol here is somewhat intricate. Morally, it is Trigorin who has slain the bird. Literally it is slain by Nina's young adorer, who has shot it, like the Ancient Mariner, in a fit of wantonness. She deserts this young man. At last she returns, and sees him again; but she will not have him, and vanishes once more into her blank existence. The sound of his pistol is heard outside the scene.

In *The Three Sisters* the refrain is different; it is the word *Moscow*. Moscow signifies the supposed brilliant life, the far-off Elysium, which haunts the fancy of the sisters, and which they never reach. Entangled by circumstance, they are left alone

146

together in the provinces. But here the refrain, as in many a ballad, is only incidental; it does not touch the vital point. The play is not merely a study in disappointment; on the contrary, a saving faith, or hope, remains, distilled from the disappointment itself. Each of the sisters expresses this in her own way, while the military music is heard without. One, who is stupidly married, exclaims that now they must live after all, must begin to live over again. The youngest exclaims that they must work for others, and that some day the human race will understand why it has suffered. To the eldest, the schoolmistress, the music seems to offer a kind of explanation; we, so she muses, shall be forgotten, but somehow our troubles will make for the happiness of those who come after us. The play ends with her cry, 'If only we could know, if only we could know!' Stated thus, the conclusion may seem unhopeful enough, or unoriginal; the force of it is only felt as the climax of a drama that has been fully acted out, in what George Eliot somewhere calls 'a troublous embroiled medium', by a crowd of characters.

In *The Cherry Orchard* the refrain is given by the title; and here the symbol is again at the true centre of the action. The imagination of each character plays about it in a different way. The orchard, a very old one, unique of its kind, and now in full flower, is seen by the spectator through most of the play. It has to be felled, and the timber will be sold, in order to pay off the debts of the owner, the lady, no longer young, who has just come home after a long absence and a stormy career. The sight of it recalls her youth; the orchard is itself a happy thing; and she says to it, 'the angels of heaven have not left *you*'. She cannot believe that it must go; she refuses to take steps that will make the sale more profitable. To her friend the merchant, Lopakhin, it is simply an asset. To the elderly student, Trofimov, it is a symbol of old Russia, which is still full of beautiful things. But it is also dreadful; for the ancient cherry-trees, in the evening, seem yet to be dreaming of the heavy days of serfdom. He reflects that Russia can only be redeemed by suffering and labour. They all go away, except the aged servant whom they have forgotten; he has the last word; he hears the sound of the axes falling.

*The Cherry Orchard* was played for the first time in Moscow, in Chekhov's presence, six months before his death; he had hastened up from Yalta to watch and advise in the rehearsals. He was applauded, honoured, and fêted to the point of exhaustion. Several of the actors have left their recollections; and we are assured that Chekhov firmly refused to consider the play a pessimistic or gloomy study of Russian life. 'It has turned out', he wrote, 'not a drama, but a comedy, almost a farce'; and this is true. The whole atmosphere is gayer and brighter, the suggestion of a decent future is less remote, than in *The Three Sisters*. The young, irrepressible Chekhov, the playwright of *The Bear* and *The Proposal*, has half revived. It would therefore be false criticism to take leave of him too solemnly.   In this play there is a governess who does silly conjuring tricks; a wonderful old uncle, who eats candy, chatters about billiards, and makes a sentimental speech to a century-old book-case; a drunken tramp who frightens a lady and requests 'thirty kopeks for a hungry Russian'; and a station-master who walks in and begins to recite a passage from Tolstoy.   There is comic love-making between a maid-servant and a clerk.   All this re-flects a gentle tint of mockery upon the sentiment itself; and yet, in Chekhov's manner, the sentiment, the deep musical theme, survives the test.   In a letter written some weeks after the performance, Chekhov advises thus, in his lighter, his native strain:

Above all, be cheerful; do not look at life so ingeniously; probably, it is in fact much simpler.   Whether it, namely, life, which we can never know, merits all the torturing reflections with which our Russian spirits wear themselves down—why, that is still the question.

And let me add a word from one of his private notebooks, which have been printed:

In the next world, I should like to be able to think this about our present life: *There were lovely visions in it.*

I do not like to end without offering a salute to the memory of that distinguished scholar, critic, and teacher, Professor Nevill Forbes.   Of his service to Slavonic studies in Britain, and especially in Oxford, much has been said by those who are entitled to

judge; and also, by those who knew him, of his
personal qualities. I am but one of many strangers
whose steps in the reading of Russian have been
guided by his books, and who can only regret that
his voice is silent.

*Accent as follows*: Alexéy Sergéevich Suvórin; Alyósha;
Amúr; Antón Pávlovich Chékhov; Azóv; Baykál; Belyáev;
Búnin; Dmítri Vasílievich Grigoróvich; Dostoévsky;
Irtýsh; Ivánov; Górky; Korolénko; Kúprin; Lopákhin;
Mélikhovo; Mikhaíl; *naródnik*; *Nóvoe Vrémya*; Ógnev *or*
Ognyóv; Ólga Leonárdovna Knípper; Sakhalín; Taganróg;
Tolstóy; Trigórin; Trofímov; Ványa; Yálta.

# Karel Čapek

## Short Tales and Fantasias

I

This artist and patriot died on Christmas Day 1938, and he was therefore spared the worst. But he had lived through the September troubles, and after Godesberg he had exclaimed, 'The world for me is dead, there is no reason for my writing any more.' Yet afterwards, in his country house among his friends, he had remarked, 'Here we are, you see, working again already!' There is a moving account of his last days and of how he went on writing while he could. A fragment has been printed of his last romance, ending in a broken sentence. It is called *The Life and Work of the Composer Foltýn*, and it contains Čapek's last work on the moral philosophy of art, a philosophy slowly evolved. The most ruinous danger, he says, for the artist, is *conceit*, or vanity: the intrusion into his work of his *ego*, which is for ever tempted to flashiness, self-display, and exaggeration. Why, the ego itself, with its unshapen experience, is just like the world without that furnishes that experience ; for in itself, it is

151

mere matter, without form and void. The watch-word of the artist, like that of the Creator, must be *Divide*! Select, reject; let the light be parted from the darkness, the waters from the waters. For this is the way of perfection; and when the dross is purged off, you may be able to rest, and to say that the work is good. You will have attained to a wider vision, a clearer understanding, and a more perfect love. Nor let us fancy that art is 'beyond good and evil'. No, it admits 'of the most exalted virtue, and also of a more repulsive viciousness and degradation than I know of in any human calling'. Čapek did not live to complete the argument, but such ideals (which are here put into the mouth of a musician) animate his best and ripest work. They explain the habit of self-suppression that marks his plays and stories and also his quest for perfection in his craft.

II

These particulars can be found in various numbers of *The Present Time* (*Přítomnost*),[n] the liberal and independent weekly published in Prague: a journal which despite the more recent muzzling restrictions still carries on courageously. Other articles treat of Čapek as a man of letters, or of his political views. He had set at the feet of Masaryk, and his *Conversations* with that very great man can now be read in English. His work is many-faceted; in the *Slavonic Review* for July 1936 there is a balanced and comprehensive sketch of it by the Czech scholar Dr. René Wellek. I am attempting no such thing, and am saying nothing of his essays, of his witty, light-handed, travel notes, or—except in passing— of his plays; but will speak only of his short stories, fantasies, and novels. Čapek earned his European fame, justly enough, by *R.U.R.*, *The Insect Play*, *The White Sickness* (translated as *Power and Glory*), and other dramas. They satirize the social order and depict, often in symbolic form, the perils that threaten it with shipwreck. Their wealth of ideas, their strength of purpose, and their pertinence to-day, must be recognized. And yet, considered as works of art, they have perils of their own. They are full of faults and fissures which will hardly stand close analysis and which are easily passed over in the theatre; and in any case, they cannot compare with the best of Čapek's stories. Most of these, though not all, have been translated [n]; but to an Englishman the author's name suggests, above all, the Robots and the Slugs, and perhaps also his horrified and humorous drawings of the London buses and posters. The stories are seldom mentioned in our critical press; although the novels of the 'trilogy' (*Hordubal*, *The Meteor*, *An Ordinary Life*) and *The First Rescue Party*, may fairly be called classics. Many of the *contes* rank with those of Chekhov or of Maupassant. There are, first and last, more than eighty of them, and it must be enough to single out a few.

## Karel Čapek

The first group of tales is included in three volumes: *Shining Deeps* (1916); *Calvaries*, or *Wayside Crosses* (literally, 'God's Suffering') (1917); and *Painful Tales* (1921). They had been preceded by a curious miscellany of anecdotes and fancies, *Krakonoš's Garden*, the work of Karel Čapek and his brother Josef, who was also his partner in *Shining Deeps* and afterwards in several of his plays. *Calvaries* is the work of Karel alone; but these two books have a common atmosphere not easy to define. They are tentative; the authors are exploring their talent, seeking for a line. They deal in delicate burlesque, or in gay Italian scenes with a background of red murder; but, above all, they are penetrated by a sense of *mystery*; and this, in its many shapes, pervades most of Karel Čapek's work in fiction. There is the passion for the unknown, the urge of the traveller to escape from home and bonds; a thirst that can never be satisfied, for there is always an enigmatical Beyond. Most of us have known men who cannot rest from travel: Are they impelled by *vis a tergo*, or by *vis a fronte*? Do they know, themselves? In *The Island*, one such wanderer is marooned among savages and takes a native mate; he longs to escape, but when the rescuers come he hides from them and cannot leave her. In *The Living Flame*, Manoel is on his deathbed, and is told to confess his sins. He has killed men, he has taken women where he could get them, and he has been all over the world, lured always by great distances, 'which frightened me like some abyss, and yet I have always rushed into them, delightedly and never wavering'. 'But what of your *sins?*' cries the priest; and departs in anger when he finds that the man does not repent at all.

A still more haunting enigma is that of Time: not the time of the clock, but real time—whatever that may be. 'Nothing is more tormenting than the present', says a speaker in *The Waiting Room*; the burden of life is that you have to wait, and 'you wait for one thing only', for 'an end to the waiting, for liberation from waiting', for some sort of painful 'deliverance', which never comes. In a little prose lyric called *The Standstill of Time*, the student at his table holds his breath in the silence of the night, which is both within him and without him; and all objects seem to him like an infinite plane surface, a sheet of linen, without time or content, and quite dead. 'And the thing that is standing still, is time'; he dare not move for fear of its 'breaking up into a thousand moments' which would 'drop down, dead as dust'. The sound of steps upon the pavement dissolves the impression, and time moves on again.

IV

The story that gives the title to the volume *Shining Deeps* reminds us, by its musical repetition, of a double theme, of De Quincey's *Vision of Sudden*

*Death*, for death and love are the themes; and they
echo in the memory of an imaginary passenger who
has survived the foundering of the '*Oceanic*' (namely,
the *Titanic*). The disaster itself is related, more
than once; and Čapek has studied the published
evidence: there is the gay scene, the growing suspense, the doom realized, the heroic bearing, the
singing of the hymn. . . . Yet the real subject is
different. There was a nameless girl on board, to
whom the traveller had never spoken, and she had
perished. She crosses and recrosses his vision; and
behold, she and no other was his ideal, and his love,
sudden and final, had lent her 'the likeness of
beauty'. After this, he cries, 'my life only *seems*
to exist, and it ends in nothing; take pity on my
soul!'

But Čapck is already evolving a new technique:
he feels the need of some definite plot, or web of
concrete circumstance, in order to heighten our
awareness of the *x*, the inscrutable factor, that lies
at the heart of it. So he begins to invent 'detective'
tales which, as Dr. Wellek observes, are of a very
unusual kind, being 'without any solution for the
mysteries; the very disappointment of our expecta-
tion is their main point'. In *The Mountain* neither
murderer nor victim is identified. The former
remains a vague bulk, a complaining voice, a somebody who is chased over the mountain by constables
and amateurs, and who is at last found dead. A
musician who has joined the party and who has
parleyed with that voice in the mist feels pity and

sympathy for the criminal, and he twangs one startling note upon his fiddle by way of symbol or of epitaph. The mystery lies not in what the matter-of-fact policemen may or may not discover but in the depths of human motive. Čapek, as will appear, was afterwards to show surprising resource in this kind of narrative.


V

In the preface to his play *The Makropulos Affair* (1922), he gallantly repudiates the charge of pessimism; the only real pessimism, he says, is defeatism—giving up hope and doing nothing. And certainly his own creed is Carlylean; it is the creed of work, and of faith in mankind. Still, some of the *Painful Tales*, published only a year previously, are overhung with gloom, and suggest the Everlasting No of *Sartor Resartus*. Every window is bricked up, every blink of hope excluded. *In the Castle* describes the fate of a governess who is in the employ of a tyrannous old count and his wife. She is bullied by them, defied by the child her pupil, and she suffers from the coarse overtures of the young handsome tutor. She plans to run away, but her unlettered mother needs her wages, and she dare not go. At last, driven to the wall and in order to get *something* out of life, she opens her door to the tutor. One night, wandering in the park, she had espied him, a nude and splendid athlete, doing his exercises. *Helena* is the story of a plain girl of twenty-five, who is drawn with bitter precision and a kind of merciless compassion. She has exalted notions, believes that there is something 'higher than love', and goes about frankly with a man older than herself rather *blasé*, who thinks her just a delightful friend. The flaw in the story is his incredible blindness to the true state of the case. In Helena there is a sudden explosion of hopeless passion. She comes to the man and confesses it, and he has to undeceive her. She is no Tatyana, but he talks to her somewhat like a bourgeois Evgeny Onegin. She goes off, they never meet again; she thinks he has done her a grievous wrong.

These are miseries of the private life; in *The Tribunal* the horizon is far wider. Čapek is often found brooding on the imperfection of human law and of legal justice. It is so indispensable, yet so rough and ready; and it never gets to the root of the matter. A young, a threefold murderer, condemned to die, is imprisoned in a hut. The president of the court-martial is troubled; on a still hoar-frosted night he listens to the pad of the guard, and hears supernal voices, which echo his own questionings. He pleads 'the law'; but he is told that 'There *is* no law!' But if there is no law, then there is no justice?—'There *is* no justice!' But if I were God, says the officer, I should *have* to judge this criminal!—The voice answers, 'There *is* no God!' Then he looks out on the country swathed in snow, sees the gleam of a bayonet, and goes to sleep 'weary and sorrowful'. Thinking, here, seems to have come to a

dead end. Does this officer speak for Čapek himself? If so, it is not the author's final mood. Let
the reader wait for the tale of *The Last Judgment*,
told below.

In *Painful Tales* Čapek has already found his
method. I cannot of course speak to the language;
but the structure, the economy and precision, are
already perfect.

VI

During the years 1921 to 1924 he produced three
of his chief plays, *R.U.R.*, *The Insect Play*, and *The
Makropulos Affair*; also the two long fantasias, *The
Absolute Factory* and *Krakatit*, which fall into the
same category. For here too all depends on some
scientific myth, or assumption, of which the results,
when it has been carried through, will be calamitous
to mankind. The assumption indeed starts with a
fact: the experts *are* to-day trying to liberate the
energy of the atom, and to make more and more
deadly explosives, just as they are making machines
more and more like Robots, or seeking to prolong
life indefinitely. It would be fatal, says Čapek, if
they were to succeed, as I will now show you;
and he makes these long, rambling novels, if such
they may be called, to prove his point. Naturally,
being written by Čapek, they are full of excellent
portraiture, of brilliant scenes, and of drastic
humour. The early romances of Mr. Wells may
well have inspired him; but he is none the less

original for that. Only, as works of art, as wholes, both these books are failures; there is something *splay*, or incoherent, in the workmanship; and we wonder what has become of the craftsman of the *Painful Tales*.

In *The Absolute Factory*, certain machines, 'Carburators', have been invented; the atomic energy has been set free; and though this is a purely physical phenomenon, it is described by a metaphysical term, the Absolute. For the Absolute penetrates all matter, and devours it; and when all the energy has been released, matter will perish and all things with it. But meanwhile, so runs the dream, the benefits will be past reckoning. Work will be needless, hunger and poverty will cease. But in fact over-production sets in, and general strife. Soldiers and statesmen contend for the secret and for the monopoly. There is a world war in which all frontiers vanish, and all races and colours, white and black and yellow, destroy one another. . . . Scenes of high comedy, in the factory or at the council table, relieve the picture. But the most incongruous feature has yet to be mentioned. Even in a dream or fantasy, our reason still wakes up revolted when we hear that the Absolute, thus conceived, is absolute reality and is identified with God. Here Čapek could not resist the opportunity of some raking satire. To get a whiff of the Absolute, as it filters through, is to be uplifted as by some strange gas, to have a vision of bliss, and to experience a religious conversion. But this does not diffuse happiness, for every church and sect claims God for itself, and religious ferocity is added to racial hatred. The Russians honour 'comrade God'; the Catholics canonize him, and try to utilize him. . . . Čapek ends with a laugh. In the end the machines are destroyed, the secret is lost, and we come away from a quiet, normal scene in a tavern.

### VII

*Krakatit*, though just as loosely put together, is a far better book. The possessor of this all-powerful explosive will be the ruler of the world, and able to extinguish mankind; hence the great powers and big business are hot upon its trail. The inventor, Prokop, who is an honest man and terrified by his own handiwork, refuses to give away the secret, in spite of many offers and temptations. He is harried, imprisoned, bullied, and at last gets free. But a treacherous associate, one Thomas, has picked up part of the formula while Prokop was delirious, and is trying to complete it. He blunders while experimenting, and blows up both himself and a whole countryside. Prokop is out of range, but his memory is shaken and he has forgotten the formula. At last he comes on a quaint old man in a cart, carrying a white mouse; and there is a quiet, idyllic ending. The old man tells Prokop that his fault had been pride, that he had attempted too much, and that now he must attempt little things, peaceful inventions that will help and not deface the world: something cheap and useful. Prokop drops into a dreamless sleep, and perceives that this wise old man was indeed God the Father, giving him the best advice. This familiar and homely style, so medieval in its piety, seems strange from the pen of a modern liberal; but we shall come on it again.

Prokop needs counsel; for, apart from his evil invention, he has something to atone for. He has had love-passages, only one of which deserves the name; and he has not behaved well. The others were wild affairs of instinct; and some of them are told in an erotic style that is really alien to Čapek. But for 'Annie' Prokop's love was genuine, and nothing Čapek ever wrote is more delicate than the opening picture. Prokop has been blown up, has staggered to her father's house and for weeks has lain as dead. One morning, half-awake, he looks up:

and there at the door stands a girl, slight and radiant, with a look of great wonder in her clear eyes, her lips parted in astonishment, and pressing some white linen to her bosom.

Then, out of some corner of the chemist's brain, comes a memory of the Sixth Odyssey; and he pours out, in the Greek, the speech of the derelict Odysseus to Nausikaa upon the sea-shore: one of the treasures of the world's poetry. '*Gunumai se, anassa.* I am thy suppliant, O queen. . . . If she is a goddess, she is like unto Artemis; if a mortal, thrice blest are her parents when they see her going to the dance. She is like the lovely young palm-tree he had seen at Delos . . . may the gods grant her her desire, a home and a husband.' . . . Then, like Odysseus, he asks for a wrap. Annie laughs, brings him a mirror, and he beholds a beard that has grown for weeks. The idyl takes its course and is at first joyous, but ends sadly. Prokop spares her innocence, but he recovers the memory of his quest, rushes off in quest of krakatit, promising in vain that he will return; and leaves her heart-broken.

All this is loosely hung upon the story, and the book, though rich in colour and comedy, remains a medley. Čapek seems, at this period, to have had some krakatit-mixture in his system, which he was fain to be rid of; and though in later years he was to return to symbolic drama and to fantasy, he now came back to his miniatures: travel notes, essays or rather *feuilletons*, talks on gardening, and little stories. In 1929–30 appeared *Tales from One Pocket* and *Tales from the Other Pocket*.

VIII

In a letter which has been printed he explains his purpose:

The kernel of *Tales from One Pocket* was the intention to write *noetic* [n] stories, about the various roads that lead to the knowledge of the truth; and so . . . the detective *genre* forced itself upon me. Here you have discoveries which are pseudo-occult, poetical, matters of routine, purely empirical, and so forth. But involuntarily, in the course of the work another *motif* came up, an ethical one, the problem of *justice*. You will find it in most of the tales of the second half of *One Pocket*. . . . The *Tales from the Other Pocket* are freer in the theme; my business there was rather to look out for flashes of tenderness and humanity in the routine of life, or of a trade, or of ordinary estimates.

But those flashes, in truth, are everywhere; Čapek cannot turn out a pocket without coming on some scrap of shining gold. This is true even of the gloomier tales, which show that he well remembered how to be 'painful'. Such is the *History of the Conductor Kalina*, in which he draws upon his memories of Liverpool. Čapek had been there in 1924; I missed him, but he supped with friends of mine. He was, they recall, merry, full of the material for his *Letters from England*, and talked about music. Seeing the new cathedral, he seemed shocked, waved his arms, and exclaimed 'A *luxus*, a *luxus*!' The musician Kalina, who knows but two words of English, and thinks in terms of sounds and noises, repeats Čapek's impressions of Merseyside: he has come to conduct a concert:

In Liverpool you have a river—I don't know its name, but it's just yellow and horrible; and this river of yours roars and resounds and bellows, howls and rattles, rumbles and trumpets, what with the ships, the tugs, the ferries, warehouses, dry docks and cranes . . . I could only see here and there a ship as tall as a church, or three fat slanting funnels. There was a stink of fish, sweating horses, jute, rum, wheat, coal, and iron: listen, when there is a big mass of iron, it has an ironish smell, quite distinct. . . .

Kalina wanders along the docks, sits down, and over

hears a fateful colloquy between a man and a woman. His musical ear perceives, simply from the voices, that the man, the 'bass-viol', is gradually persuading the woman, the 'clarinet', to acquiesce in some dreadful deed. They move off; he rushes about wildly, through the night; tries to inform the police, who only smile and convoy him to his hotel. Next day he conducts his concert, and from headlines in the papers he learns one more English word. 'I think', he concludes, 'that "Murder" signifies *Vražda.*'

All of us, at least all professors of literature, read detective tales, good and otherwise; and are ready to resent the device of withholding the solution and baulking the suspense. But with Čapek, as I have said, it is no mere trick of the trade; it is his method of throwing into relief the inscrutable element in human nature. He uses it most flexibly, for humorous or tragic ends. In one dark story, *Oral Confession*, a priest, a lawyer, and a doctor in turn hear, under the seal of professional secrecy, and from the same man, a recital that leaves them cold with horror; we are never told what it is. He does not want shrift or advice, but comes only to relieve his mind; and he dies in hospital, when the doctor has given him an extra dose of morphia. 'You were very *nice* to him,' says the priest; 'at least he did not suffer.'

The most deeply imagined of these tales is perhaps the magnificent *Last Judgment*. It expresses Čapek's feeling that there is *no* Last Judgment, ultimate and divine. Kugler, a ninefold murderer, after being at last shot dead, finds himself in the next world, before a court which is just like an earthly court, with three morose old men presiding. 'For reasons that will soon appear, the Cross on which witnesses take the oath was missing.' There was only one witness, a tall old man in a blue cloak, who is heard with a mixture of deference and impatience; often he seems to the court to ramble. He is God, the supreme Truth-Teller; he knows everything; and he tells Kugler the details of each of his murders, and their consequences. How a daughter of one of his victims went to the bad; how he had killed a married couple for their money, but had missed it, and all the time it was under the bed. . . . Kugler is much interested, and reminds Omniscience of a tenth murder, which had not been mentioned. No, says God, *that* man had recovered and is alive; he is an informer, no doubt,—but he is kind-hearted and fond of children. God knows too much to be a judge, he can only be a witness; for even in heaven, it is only *men* who can pass judgement—human judgement. The court returns, condemns Kugler to hell 'for the term of his life', and calls the next case. There is no mystery here about the facts,— on the contrary. But *we* have to pronounce upon them, and yet—how dare we do so?

Some of the lighter tales are more in the style of Mr. Chesterton. There is the housebreaker who unluckily had left the print of his denture in the dust; or the victim who had inexplicably vanished;

he had been wrapped up in one of his own carpets and despatched by rail. Or there is the priceless Eastern carpet which an enthusiast tries to steal. He breaks in at night, but is baffled by the cat Amina, who sits upon it and gives the alarm. One pleasing and humane story is *The Case of the Child*. A mother leaves her baby unattended for a moment in the street. It disappears, and the police have no clue, for it is like a hundred other babies and she cannot describe it; can only babble fond words about it. At last it is traced. It had been stolen by a poor unmarried girl, who had been bereaved of her own infant and who wanted one to nurse. The first mother identifies her baby, and rewards the girl handsomely.

IX

For all his gravity, Čapek can cast it off quickly enough. He is at his gayest when he writes for children of all ages, about wizards and birds with seven heads and comic detectives and frogs and quack doctors. All these figure in his *Nine Tales* (translated as *Fairy Tales*), which were published in 1930 just after the *Pocket Stories*, and which are illustrated by Josef Čapek's drawings. These, like Thackeray's in *The Rose and the Ring*, are artfully artless and exactly hit their mark. So too are Karel Čapek's own, which are to be found in his *Dashenka* (1931), the life history of a real puppy, where they are accompanied by real photographs. Both these books are becoming familiar to English readers, and ought to have a long life. In the *Dog Story*, Josef supplies the picture of the white, half-transparent fairy dogs, graceful elongated creatures dancing and singing by night in a silvery meadow. They are seen by a real puppy who is finding his way home alone; and he knows they are not of this world, for they never scratch or hunt for fleas, and the stems of the grass do not stir under them. Then an old fairy dog tells how the primal dogs were restless, because they craved for a god that they could *smell*; and God answered their prayer, and made them up a god, who was man, out of the bones of many animals that were brought to him by the suppliants. Thus man has the qualities of the lion, the camel, and the cat, and the 'magnanimity of the horse'. But no dog will carry the bones of another dog; and so man has 'not the fidelity of the dog, no, not the fidelity of the dog!' In another tale cat and dog, after some misunderstandings, can fraternize and divide their labour. One can see in the dark and climb, the other can bark and smell; and together, like two policemen, they are seen rounding up a robber.

Čapek likes cats, and tries to penetrate their minds. In his book of brief *feuilletons*, *Of Intimate Things*, pussy appears three times. Beware, says the author, of being sentimental over the *wrong* mystery. Do not think, when her kittens have been taken from her and she is restless, that she is grieving. No, her behaviour, her postures, are just what they would have been had the kittens still been there. This is only nature's mechanism, unchanging through the generations; it is not a sign of emotion at all, but just a force driving from behind. The human mother is different; *she* is creative, she has initiative, has to learn her business every time; and this is the work of intellect. (Ah, where did she acquire that gift of freedom?) 'Get out, silly puss, we don't understand each other any longer!'

Elsewhere we learn what the cat really thinks of us. He trusts us, for one thing. When he was wild in the jungle he trusted, and he still will trust, no other cat. We all know about pussy's egoism and his detachment; but in *The Cat's Point of View* Čapek gives a new turn to this commonplace:

The thing there is My Man. I do not fear him. . . . He is not beautiful, for he has no fur. Not having enough saliva, he has to wash himself with water. He mews harshly and far more than he need. . . . *Open the door for me!* . . . In My rooms, he preserves cleanliness.

Pussy watches the author digging into white leaves with a sort of black claw—'he can't play in any other way'. The man has no pleasures, he never sings for love, and sometimes he stops playing, and then pussy is sorry for him and is embraced by him, and in the man 'a gleam of a higher life awakens'. But then pussy goes out into the night on his own affairs, 'to listen to the dark voices'.

# Karel Čapek

## Later Novels

### I

Čapek now reverted from the short story to the novel, and published (1933-5) three volumes, of which only the last, *An Ordinary Life*, is of any length. *The Meteor* is really three distinct tales bound together, while its predecessor, *Hordubal*, is a tale with a sequel, the latter being in quite a different key. Once more there is a murder; and the victim, Hordubal, is an unlettered peasant who has returned, after a long absence, from America, with a bag of hard-earned dollars, to rejoin his wife. He has few words; but his mental soliloquies, with their doublings-back and in all their inconsequence, are given with wonderful skill. As he approaches his village he dreams of his cows and of his plans and of his welcome. But it is what Tennyson calls an iron welcome. His wife, Polana, is cold, she is petrified when he appears. She has become the mistress of an insolent, horsy servant, Stephen, who now rules the house. There also is Hordubal's child Hafie; but she prefers Stephen to the newly

170

arrived father,—upon whom the facts slowly dawn.
He wanders alone in the uplands, where there is
only earth and sky and the sound of cattle-bells;
and the wind, which is flying by like time itself.
He sees far below him two figures, the man and the
woman, small as ants and close together. . . . He
talks to an old shepherd; he buys a philtre from a
gipsy, but in vain. The village is up in arms over
the scandal, and he is made to feel his disgrace. To
stop their tongues, he first betrothes Hafie to
Stephen—a Zolaesque touch; and then, when this
makes things worse, he breaks the arrangement and
packs the fellow off. More complications follow,
but at last Hordubal falls ill, takes to his bed, and
is there found, in the closely barred house, mur-
dered. Some instrument has been driven through
his heart.

With this discovery the sequel opens, and the subject is now the criminal procedure: the search by
the police, and the trial of Stephen and Polana. The
narrative becomes objective and lucid; the inarticulate Hordubal, with his imaginings, is no more.
Čapek here lays on his colours thickly. For Polana
is near her time, and owing to the dates Hordubal
could not be the father of the coming child. All
the women regard her without mercy. Hafie, in
the simplest manner, bears witness in court to the
intrigue. Stephen, in a useless burst of decency,
confesses and exonerates Polana. But he receives a
life sentence, and she is condemned to 'heavy
imprisonment' for twelve years. All the portraiture

here is admirable; there are the advocates; the old policeman who knows his village and is willing to let the case slide, and the young one who ferrets out the facts; and the two doctors who differ—was Hordubal shot, or was he stabbed with a certain 'basket-needle'? Can he have died naturally, and *then* been stabbed? Was the motive love, or the money that has been missing and at last found? The answers are left open, though the verdict is certain; and Čapek leaves us contemplating the unsolved problems.

## II

In *The Meteor*, the unknown quantity has a different artistic value. As in *The Mountain*, there is a victim whose name and history are untraceable; but there is no question of crime. An unknown airman has been wrecked and is dying in a hospital. The setting is natural, even matter of fact, in contrast with the three stories that are panelled into it. There is 'an odour of carbolic, coffee, tobacco, and humanity'. The doctors, intent only on their job, are not imaginative, and form the somewhat impatient audience. Then three persons, a sister of mercy, a 'clairvoyant', and a poet, in turn relate the imaginary life-story of the patient. They have no facts to go upon, and each narrative is a revelation of the teller. The sister dreams on conventional lines. She supposes the airman to have fled from an unhappy home, to have betrayed a noble girl and quitted her and wandered to the tropics, and to have been at last conscience-stricken. He has flown homewards to find her and to make amends, but has foundered on the way.

The clairvoyant's tale, like *Krakatit*, is full of wild adventure, and like it turns upon the loss of a chemical, or physical, formula of vast significance. It has been rejected by the authorities; and the discoverer, losing heart, flies to the Antilles and lies long in a state of mental stagnation. Much time passes; but one day he sees something in a professional journal which drives him to fly back and recover his priceless notes lest they should be stolen.

The poet's tale is richer, more violent in colouring, and still more inventive. Again the flier is an exile, and again we are with him in the Antilles. A blow on the head has suspended his memory; he forgets his name, and all the past. He is harboured by a rascally sugar-planter, who tries to make use of him, and with whose daughter he falls in love. In order to win her and to force the father to consent, he sets up as a rival in big business. He discovers a lake of hot asphalt, of untold value; and he suffers (here Čapek the fantast is in his glory) from hardship, from his sullen negro workmen, from parasites,—and from disappointment. For the big business men will not finance his discovery, or look at it; it would break their monopoly. He despairs and is in evil case. But one day, while writing to the girl, he suddenly remembers his name and his childhood, and flies off to claim his inheritance.

In a long subtle prelude the poet had discoursed on the nature of 'fantasy', or imagination, and of its relationship to real life. It is untrammelled; it can range over every possibility—and the real is just *one* of a thousand possibilities. But its task of the artist is to choose the *most* possible among them all; and this may, or may not, answer to the actual facts. Nor does the imagination consciously invent; like a dog upon the trail, it does not know what it will find, or by what pathway, after many a false start, it will arrive. The poet, or inventor (*Dichter*) must let the dog lead him, as 'necessity' may prescribe. '*What* that necessity is, do not ask him—ask God!' In passing the poet lets fall one profound remark:

> I am trying to excuse literature for its love of the tragic and the ridiculous. Both of these are *détours* invented by fantasy in order to create the illusion of reality, by its own methods, and its own unreal paths. *Reality itself is neither tragical nor ridiculous: it is too serious, too infinite, to be either the one or the other.* Sympathy and laughter are merely the shocks that accompany and pronounce upon external events.

The poet is doubtless speaking for the author; have we here Čapek's *apologia* for his own discursive habit, visible in stories like *Krakatit* ? However this be, the poet had begun his tale by piecing together the scraps of information available—the tropical coins in the sick man's pocket, etc., before he lets his fancy loose. The doctors, at the same time, try to guess from his morbid symptoms from what

region he has come.   On the last page, they discover
something, but not much; the nameless dead man,
they hear, had been registered in Paris as a Cuban.


III

The unknown quantity here was not only the
identity of the airman but the pathway and the goal
of the poet's imaginings.   In *An Ordinary Life* the
mystery is different.   Čapek, for a time, abandons
such effects, and all that is sensational and adven-
turous.   He explores the inner consciousness,
brought to light by reflection, of an average man,
who is outwardly—and also in his own opinion—
commonplace.   We never even hear his name; he
is Anybody.   Only, nobody *is* an average man!
He is a retired, successful station-master, who knows
that he is mortally ill and that he will never see
another spring blossom in his garden.   The keynote
of his life and character has been *order*, method and
regularity: the words recur like a symbol.   He
has gone straight along the railway-track of life,
and now it is carrying him off into the infinite.
First of all he tells a straightforward story, tells it
admirably; it is a small masterpiece.   His memory
is infallible.   He describes his home and childhood;
his father the rough kindly joiner, his sensitive
mother, and he knows what qualities he has inherited
from each of them.   He recalls a village funeral:
how the dead man had suddenly become important;
how the child had wondered why any corn-chandler,

175

or furrier, should be buried just like a king; and had wished that he, the child, could head the procession himself. Soon he has glimpses of cruelty and sensuality in others. He struggles through school, and blunders through college and has to quit it. He is put to serve in a railway office in the city; but he falls ill and is packed off for his health to an up-country station at 'the end of the world'. He is now on the railroad of life and his true career begins. He is promoted from station to station; and each of these is carefully vignetted: the curious 'characters', the atmosphere, remain distinct. On the way he has loved and married, and has been left a childless widower. Once, during the War, he had been master at a big junction, and like a good Czech had used his position to sabotage the traffic of the Austrian. Later he had found himself in the ministry of railways at Prague, a person of consequence. He spends his last days in writing down his chronicle. It could not be bettered, it could be printed by itself; but it is not all. For he has been visited, as he wrote, by strange reflections. This common story, after all, was unique; and why? He becomes aware of some mysterious, disquieting *hinterland*, which must be explored. He had, for instance, dreamed of organizing a *perfect* railway station; and this preoccupation had drawn him away, as he had dimly felt at the time, from his wife. She had become inured to the fact; and in compensation she had made for him, had imposed upon him, a special routine of comfort which was like a fetter.

176

So, in the sequel, he begins all over again, with a quickened self-consciousness, and digs deeper. He speaks at length; but we are not bored by the repetition; indeed the story renews its life. He knows nothing of philosophy; he does not talk about the 'censor' and the 'id'. In another story, Čapek derides a professor who chatters about 'repressed ideas'. But like Launcelot Gobbo, the old man hears two voices debating within him, two egos,—two at least. The first is his normal, somewhat complacent self; the second is the critic, the self-distruster, who makes out a damaging case against the first. It detects the seeds of vanity, and even of perversion, sown in childhood; and also the vulgar ambitions of the climber. True, he had not been unfaithful to his good wife; but did he not sometimes *hate* her (*odi et amo*)? and he *could* have broken the chain of silk, *could* have gone with a gipsy girl. . . . Well, what principle, what 'order' was there in all this? Going deeper, he comes on many more egos—the hypochondriac, the romantic, the solitary, the patriot, even the poet. He had once made some bad verses and forgotten them; a young admirer comes in and reminds him of them. He is sorry that they are dead verses—for at least they were an attempt to express his vision of palm-trees.—But what kind of a drama was this? The curtain is coming down on all these selves, and the play seems to have no solution.

But he has a glimpse of one at last. There *is* a real, a single self,—single just because it is manifold. He thinks of his forbears and of their presence in his blood, and he seems to talk with them—and also with his never born, his possible brothers; he feels that he might have been any one of these. Indeed, he might have been anybody in the world. Whitman-like he feels one with his kind, with the postman in the street, or the boy who passes with his girl. Even his enemy is 'dreadfully near to him'; and the closer he comes to these others, 'the more he finds himself'. 'I am whatever I am capable of comprehending.' And this, he adds,

is the true ordinary life, this most ordinary life of all: not that which is mine, but that which is *ours*, the immeasurable life of us all. We are all ordinary, since there are so many of us; and yet—it is all so glorious! Maybe God too is a quite ordinary life; only, the thing is to see and recognize him.

He ends with a vision of a station, with its lamps and its rattling, and a little girl at a window putting out her tongue, and the train going off, off, as he will soon be doing himself.

Čapek in his epilogue to the trilogy enlarges upon this conception. We are reminded of the tale, told above, of *The Last Judgment*; except that here no one is judged. Truth, he insists, is multiple; and the judgement of good and evil is relative to each observer. Yet we shall find a harmony between all those voices if we will but look within; for there at least we are at home; and so we shall understand our fellow-men, our equals. 'Even the most ordinary life is infinite; the value of each soul is illimitable.' Čapek seems to have accepted none of the current creeds; but he speaks as a humanist, and comes to this conclusion by his own path. The gentle setting of his story is all in keeping. At the outset, the dead man's young doctor talks with an elderly neighbour who is pruning in his garden, and tells how he had come by the manuscript. At the close, when it has been read, they discuss it while they gossip about the garden. The neighbour says, 'Poor fellow! . . . Such a nice, *regular* man.'

v

The political shocks and tremors of recent years left their mark on Čapek, and he swung back once more from portraying the interior life to prophesying a world-calamity. *The War with the Newts*, or Salamanders, came out in 1936. The book shows no little waste of power, and for once Čapek can, at times, be even tiresome. There is a mass of pseudo-zoology on the anatomy and 'sexual life' of the newts; a chapter on long business meeting, in which a company debates how to exploit them; and much press-clipping, printed in a motley of types, showing them as the natural prey of the journalist. There is indeed much fun and high spirits in these extracts; Čapek has something schoolboyish in his composition—almost as if he were an Englishman! One reporter describes the mad, savage dance of the

179

newts, pacing and wriggling as though round an altar; 'but there is no altar there, and no god':

I know this description looks pretty mechanical; but if you add to it the chalky pallor of the moonlight and the long steady murmur of the tide, it had something about it that was magical beyond measure, and a kind of bewitchment.

The whole overture, on the other hand, is admirable. Captain Van Toch and his team of half-breeds may owe something to Conrad; but soon we are in a world of fable. Water-creatures with small semi-human hands, big heads and fishlike tails, who at first can only say 'ts, ts', and who feed on the insides of sea-shells that are full of pink pearls. . . . These newts are a great invention, and might have delighted Swift. First-rate, too, is the interview of the Captain with the millionaire whom he persuades to finance his venture; and his covenant with the newts, that he will bring a diver to kill the sharks who prey upon them. The creatures learn to talk and perform; we meet them in a zoo, and in a travelling show. They are educated, up to a point; they learn a 'basic English'; they are fed, and utilized, and insured, and enslaved. The churches are perplexed. The Catholics say that they cannot be baptized, not being of the seed of Adam; they have no original sin that can be purged away. The Protestants make a simplified Bible for them 'on waterproof paper'. But all this is a prelude to the War. It is foreseen by the old doorkeeper Mr. Povondra, whose hobby it is to collect the press cuttings.

The war is triply internecine, when it comes: men against men, men against newts, and at last newts against newts. Čapek, with all his gusto, narrates the horrors. The scenes of carnage multiply. Each of the Great Powers has its own regiments of Salamanders, and the satirist mocks impartially the Briton, the Frenchman, and the German (who needs, for *his* newts, more 'living-room'). It is a German pessimist, Meynert, who sees what is coming: the newts will arise and destroy their masters; and this they do, although an English pamphleteer would have them extirpated by a new League of Nations. For the newts, like beavers, are great dam-builders, and they too need living-room in shallow water; and they proceed to 'enlarge the sea', and erode the land. Hence a series of appalling earthquakes all over the world. There is a conference, which of course breaks down, between the men and the newts (who have chartered human delegates to speak for them). The final catastrophe approaches; and old Mr. Povondra, fishing in Prague, sees a newt's head bobbing up in the Vltava. Here the author breaks off, and debates within himself how the story shall end. Probably the newts will rule the earth, form states, almost eliminate mankind, and repeat man's faults and blunders; and then—die out. A few men may slink back from their refuges, and 'all will be as before'. There will be a new fable about a Deluge, 'sent down by God for the sins of the race'. And what next?—The author does not know.

VI

What is his drift, in this somewhat confused piece of satire? Many threads are interwoven; we can unravel two or three. First, society, by an inherent law, is heading for self-destruction, what with economic forces, the unconscionable progress of science, universal armament, and the general lust for power. Secondly, the inferior races, exploited by the white ones, will out-multiply them and will at last turn and rend them. These are familiar fears. More subtle is the conception of the newt, when he is fully developed and in power. In the mass, he is irresistible; but this is just because he is of a mean and dreary type. Čapek thus prefigures a future race of men, all equal, all homogeneous, and all alike, who will get on, in the words of the croaker Meynert, 'without philosophy, without the life after death, and without art'. They will be horribly *average*, cries the English Mr. X; who, says the author, 'is partly myself'.

'They have taken from human civilization only what is common, utilitarian, mechanical, and repetitive . . . and left out all in it that was aimless and sportive, all play of fancy, everything antique' . . . and their disposition is therefore 'cold and brutal'.

Čapek is an honest thinker; and in this book, imperfect as a work of art, he does not pretend to find a solution. He points out a danger; his nightmare is a perpetual cycle of events, with a tendency always to the worse. The Europe of those years,

1934–6, might well cause bad dreams. Still, he had not finished; and presently appeared *The First Rescue Party*, the last of his completed novels, and the nearest of them all to perfection.

VII

The nearest, because he seems here to have felt the call to the artist to make sacrifices (*entbühren sollst!*),—to divide and select; it is the ordinance, which I quoted at the outset, of his musician Foltýn. There is no fantasy, no picture of an inverted and calamitous Utopia; no sociology; and no profound talk about the ego. It is a plain straightforward tale of heroic adventure, and a picture of men and manners. Many might have thought of the bare plot; the virtue lies in the telling, and to this a pale summary can do no justice. The method so far resembles that of *Hordubal*, that there is much of what I have called mental soliloquy; though the boy of seventeen, Stanislas or Standa Půlpan, in whom the story centres, is much more articulate than the unlettered Hordubal. He does not tell the tale; it is told for him, or rather through him, through his observations, thoughts and feelings. We learn everything from his quick wits and sharp unjaded senses:—his fears, his vanity, his blunders, his day-dreams, and his fundamental courage. Standa is throughout the chorus and interpreter. The miners his comrades are for the most part uneducated, and they talk, if at all, in their own idiom.

Much of the book is dialogue; and the result is a masterly gallery of portraits, often self-portraits, with Standa in the midst of them, the most distinct of all.

VIII

This lad of seventeen comes of a mining family; but he has had five tedious years in a *Realschule*, and two in an architect's office, learning to be a draughtsman; and he can talk some German. A commercial disaster breaks off his course, and he finds himself in a coal-mine, on the lowest rung of the ladder, filling and shoving the trucks. Lonely and bullied, he has visions which he keeps to himself: how one day he will be important, will speak and contend for the underpaid and underrated pitmen; how meantime he will do gallant deeds and win much praise. This last dream, we shall find, comes true. One of the band, a superior man, Hansen the engineer, befriends him; and Standa adores Hansen, and also, very far off, his wife Helga. But he is lodging with another of the miners, the strange melancholy Adam, who has a beautiful wife, and the boy is vaguely aware of something amiss in the *ménage*. We hear of his adolescent fancies, in which both women figure; but these are banished, for the time, by the news of a disaster.

There has been an explosion in the Kristina pit; many have been injured, and three men are down there still, buried alive. There is a call for volunteers; the first rescue party is to be made up; and Standa, quaking, but impelled he knows not why, rushes forward and is the first to offer. They look askance on this puny intruder, but he is allowed to go. There are seven in the party: besides Adam and Hansen, there is the kindly carpenter Martínek; the slow-witted giant, Matula the mason; 'grand-papa' Suchánek, the feeblest but wisest of the band; and the little Pepek, the most vocal, with a wicked tongue, inquisitive and troublesome, yet tough as whipcord, fearless, and at bottom friendly. Lastly there is the overseer Jan Andres, known as the Dog, unpopular and efficient, the leader of the party, who gives his orders like a drill-sergeant. Plenty of chances here for altercation, when they go down to risk their lives. They volunteer, not like Standa in youthful ardour, but as a matter of business, to earn the extra pay for their children, or as an everyday duty; the three prisoners 'must not be left there'. Nothing heroic, they protest, about that.

## IX

Standa goes down with them on two successive days; and these chapters occupy about one-fifth of the book; the rest of the story passes above ground. But those fifty pages are packed very close; and Čapek may or may not have studied Zola's imposing and weighty *Germinal*. However this be, he too is 'realistic', minute and documentary. The pages bristle with technical terms and miners' slang; there are many words unmeet for ladies—but it is all 'clean dirt'. Čapek's hand is lighter than Zola's, and he does not go on so long. Some of the scenes are superb: the thin, ungrown boy admiring the torsos of the others as they wash; the old grandpapa, buried under a downfall, dragged out, and clamouring to go back into danger for his lantern and his hammer; and the terrors of Standa when his lamp goes out and he is alone in the darkness. He escapes; but to his chagrin, just as they hear the three prisoners knocking, the second party, the relief, arrives, and is likely to get all the credit. The first party go up in the cage, and adjourn to an inn to celebrate the day. A scene follows that might have pleased Fielding. Delicate points arise over the ceremonial of drinking. Who shall have the honour of drinking first? Mr. Hansen the engineer, of course. But what about the Dog, Andres the overseer, who is arriving later? Shall *he* be honoured too? They decide, after debate, that he shall; but Matula declines to drink *after* him. He enters, and is asked, not harshly but as a matter of interest, *why* he is a Dog? He is told why: he is too rigid, he does not allow them enough rope; and he defends himself, not ineffectively, and points to his war record. They talk of their wives, and speculate, in plain terms, about the relationship of the Adams. They all know that the couple have never been really mated, and they set this down to Adam's humility and timidity in the presence of his idolized wife. Old Suchánek, not without reason, warns Standa to keep his distance with the lady and to change his lodging.

Next day the tale is in the papers, and he rushes round to tell the comrades; but they care little for the news, and prefer to show off their children to him; we see each interior, trim or slatternly. One thing stays in Standa's memory, and we hear Čapek's deeper note. Adam is hanging little coloured glass balls on his rose-bushes, and the contorted figures of the two men are mirrored in them. It is amusing; but Standa does not want to laugh, and he reflects:

What peculiarly poor creatures we are, both of us! what a crooked and ridiculous sort of reflection it would be if I were now to take Adam's arm, and say to him, 'Adam, it is awful, but I am in love with your wife!' What should we both look like, in that ball?

They all go down, for the second time, and are met with bad reports of gas. They reach the spot where the second party had taken over the work, and they put on their masks. Adam looks like a lean man wearing an elephant's trunk. There is a fall from above, and Martínek has a bad knock, but insists on going on. The heavy gas has not yet risen waist-high. Then Standa, the inexperienced, puts his fingers in the woodwork, and they are crushed; he faints, is carried off by Red Cross men, taken up in the cage, and brought to hospital. He will never descend the pit again. The hospital scenes relieve the stress, though he has to lose some of the finger-joints of the left hand. The operation succeeds, and the old surgeon comforts him by showing the stumps that *he* had lost through the Röntgen rays—and yet he does his work! Helga Hansen, the happy wife, brings roses, talks of her husband, kisses Standa, and goes. He reads the day's news, and is ashamed and disgusted that he, the clumsy one, should be styled a 'youthful hero', while the real workers are ignored. He has by now purged away much of his conceit. Next he hears that he has been noticed in official quarters, that he is to go back to his office and be well looked after and finish his studies. He learns that it is the comrades themselves who have made friendly representations. Alas, thinks he, he will now drift gradually away from them, and be lonelier than ever. Martínek reports to him how the band had again gone to the inn, had sung and danced and wrestled and been jolly. They are to go down next day for the third time; the rescue has not yet been effected.

x

And next day, in bed, Standa pictures their doings and the scene: the heavy evil air and the dangers, and himself still pushing the trucks. He imagines himself telling Adam what he now knows to be the truth, that Marie adores her husband and is only waiting for a word from him. In his excitement, Standa imagines a crash, a fall; and after extracting leave from the doctor, hurries off to the

gate of the pit.   He hears that there has been a bad
collapse, and that one man, No. 192, has 'remained
there'.   Pepek comes, tells him that this was—
Adam; describes Adam's bravery, and how nothing
could have been done for him; but

> we put the lamps in a row, that they might shine, as it were,
> on Adam's last journey; and grandpapa Suchánek prayed
> in the name of us all, in miner fashion. . . .   Adam had a
> fine funeral.

And, adds Pepek, 'it was a *good* party', though there
was nothing 'heroic' in what they did.
    This is the end.   After a fit of crying Standa
feels that he is now a man, though still solitary, and
he has a sense of 'calm, reconciliation, courage,—or
something'.   Čapek, like Chekhov, well knows
where to stop.   It is all very like life, which has to
go on.   A new volume opens for the boy, though
not for the comrades; and Adam will never know
that his wife loved him.   The three prisoners have
perished.
    In Čapek's narrative art a kind of rhythm can be
detected.   The earlier brief stories are succeeded
by the big, fantastic canvases, which he can scarcely
manage.   A book like *Krakatit*, in its violent
passages, reminds an English reader of the old
painter John Martin, who a century ago splashed
his torrid colours on his pictures of Herculaneum
or of the Deluge.   Then came the host of shorter
tales, of far finer make; and then the 'trilogy',
culminating in *An Ordinary Life*, with its close

workmanship, restraint, and subdued style. Then one more fantasy; and the novel which has just been described, done in his best and most concentrated manner. Čapek was now at the summit of his powers, and he died at the age of forty-eight.

# Reason and Enthusiasm in the Eighteenth Century

## I

No one could feel the honour of lecturing in the University of Manchester, and on this foundation, more keenly than a former colleague and friend of Robert Adamson. *Sunt aliquid Manes.* Some of us can still hear and see him, it may be nearly thirty years ago, speaking in this Theatre on Giordano Bruno, and opening amid a puzzled silence. Sternly he recited, in his strong voice, the text of the martyr's condemnation by the Holy Office. Adamson's modest mastery of his theme, his ardour for the exact truth, and the masonry of his squared and chiselled sentences, were all characteristic. We know that he was a born historian of thought, and that through the history of thought he moved towards that original and constructive effort which we have, despite his early death, in something more than outline. No one could have spoken so well on the subject that I choose to-night—one of the many revulsions, in the so-called age of prose, against the dominant genius of that age. There is one excuse for a person of letters, who is but a reader of philosophy, embarking on those waters; namely, that Adamson himself was deeply concerned and conversant with letters. He knew, indeed, and loved well the works of pure art; but he moved with special ease in the borderland between the works of art and the productions of abstract thought. He was for ever watching how ideas translate themselves into human terms and passions, and so into form, and how they mould, by repulsion indeed as often as by attraction, the minds of the unphilosophical. How he might have judged the conflict that I am to sketch, between the spirit of reason and what was then called 'enthusiasm', it would be improper to guess; but we may be sure that reason, in his hands, would have lost none of her rights, and that he would also have been awake to the enduring vitality of something in human nature which eighteenth-century reason was ready to repudiate. I remember him one day pointing to the people coming out of a chapel, and saying in his dispassionate way, '*That* will last a very long time.' He meant, I think, that 'that' was, after all, a manifestation of the spirit, or reason, which constituted all things. Such an idea, at any rate, is in accord with Adamson's earlier line of thought.

II

It is not necesssary here to go into the abstruser senses of the term *reason*. We all have an idea, sufficient for the contrast now to be drawn, of what it meant in the time of the 'Enlightenment'. To Locke, reason is the master-faculty which apprehends the disagreement or agreement of ideas; to Hume, those 'ideas' are themselves but feebler copies of the sensations (in his parlance 'impressions') which recur in memory. To Kant, afterwards, Reason meant a faculty of an order superior to the mere logical understanding. But to this understanding we allude—deductive or inductive, and ending in an abstract universal proposition—when we say that reason dominates an age. Reason, so understood, tends to be regarded as the supreme guide to truth in all departments; as checking, and approving, if not always as exclusively furnishing, the data of truth, and more especially of truth philosophical and theological. It is in this latter field that the clash between reason and *enthusiasm* comes out sharply.

A better name for the spirit of reason is the *critical* spirit, whose working forms the stuff of intellectual history at all times, but above all at the time which we are considering: which is, roughly, the century between the English Revolution and the French. It is the spirit whose absence or presence makes the gulf between 1640 and 1740, between *Religio Medici* and the essays of Hume; or, taking later dates, between Bossuet's *Histoire Universelle* and the work of Gibbon. The critical spirit, through creeks and inlets making, and also with many a temporary ebb, comes gradually to apply itself to

every order of facts: in the regions of physical
science, scholarship, exegesis, history, and theology.
At first it is negative and destructive. In the hands
of its pious founder, or earliest great champion,
Pierre Bayle, it seeks to destroy historical and biographical legend, classical and Hebrew mythology.
The sceptical movement in religion is thus only one
element, though a very big one, in this ubiqui-
tous process, which is still sometimes called the
Enlightenment, or *Aufklärung*—a name originally
given by sympathizers. But the critical spirit only
demolished in order to build. The great construc-
tions of Gibbon and Adam Smith are amongst its
fruits in Britain. But I am not treating here of
history or learning. Reason, or the critical spirit,
in the form of plain daylight sense, appears not only
in the philosophical reaction of Reid and other
realists, but in the more worldly writers. It binds
together works as different as the essays of Johnson,
the letters of Chesterfield, the novels of Fielding,
and the memoirs of Horace Walpole. The cult of
reason is commended by Chesterfield with unusual
fervour:

Use and assert your own reason; reflect, examine, and
analyse everything, in order to form a sound and mature
judgement; let no οὗτος ἔφα impose upon your understanding,
mislead your judgement, or dictate your conversation. Be
early what, if you are not, you will, when too late, wish you
had been. Consult your reason betimes; I do not say that it
will always prove an unerring guide; for human reason is
not infallible; but it will prove the least erring guide that you
can follow. Books and conversation may assist it; but

adopt neither, blindly and implicitly; try both by that best rule, which God has given to direct us, Reason. Of all the troubles do not decline, as many people do, that of thinking. (Feb. 7, 1749.)

What reason, in this context, exactly signifies, it is easier to feel than to define; but we can get nearer to the meaning by noting to what temper of mind it is alien or hostile. One such opposite, with which we are not now concerned, is the quickening spirit of the new poetry, from Collins to Blake; and in Blake's aphorisms the protest against reason attains its height. But another opposite is *enthusiasm*, in the peculiar sense of the term then current.

The rational spirit, as we know, thinks rather than dreams or feels; feeling, at least, has to pass its scrutiny, and has to be sensible. Reason sees the world in line rather than in colour; there is no rainbow fringe to its lens. It is, or was (to add a commonplace), hostile to the undefined and transcendental, and to the sense of mystery. Poets like Pope or Crabbe or Canning never seem to be surprised at anything, except at what they think unreason. The well-known label, the 'renascence of wonder', covers a fragment of this phenomenon. And there are moods in which it is a comfort, allied perhaps to the advance of years, to get back from that 'renascence' and from the romantic writers to the cool daylight of their predecessors, and to what Mr. Saintsbury calls the 'peace of the Augustans'—a peace we must remember, which was often furiously troubled. But this is only a personal view. What we need never forget is the profound streak of the mystical and transcendental at the very heart of the rational age, outside as well as inside poetry and art. We have but to think of Berkeley's last work, *Siris*, with its dive into the neo-Platonists; or of the later works of William Law, when he looked into the abysses of Boehme; or of his companions, who are so well described by Miss Spurgeon in the *Cambridge History of English Literature*. Both Law and Berkeley, deeply pious men, had begun as votaries of reason and dialectic, with a strong dash of satire, and both of them afterwards plunged into mysticism. In Burke we have a kind of middle position; he does not court such adventures, and he believes that all which *we* cannot understand nevertheless lies in clear light to the divine reason. Yet he is full of the feeling of awe for the unexplained power which lies behind the presence of man upon the earth and behind the social fabric that ties the generations together. All these forces, qualifying the reign of pure logic and good sense, are only now named to show that *enthusiasm*, presently to be defined, is no isolated thing, but is simply one manifestation of an impulse of revolt, surging up independently in many minds, against the ruling temper.

All these *protesters*, who dealt in romantic verse or philosophic mysticism, though fairly abundant, were very much on their defence throughout the hundred years we are regarding. The future was with them, but no one could clearly see that. If the world had come to an end in 1780, Britain, on the whole, would have gone to her account in her old age with a record for the poetry of satire, argument, and manners, for the novel of manners, for rationalistic philosophy and utilitarian theology. There would have been great exceptions, but exceptions they would have been. Enthusiasm was perhaps the greatest of all; and it was ever on its defence, and knew it well. To-day, I believe, it is reason and logic that are thought to be in the dock; and before closing I shall suggest a modest unprofessional defence of them.

### III

It will not, I hope, be tedious to resort for a few moments to the dictionaries, and harp on the usage of the word enthusiasm and of its derivatives. Light may be thrown on the history of opinion by hunting down a word which begins as a term of praise, becomes for a century a term of contempt and distrust, and then regains some, though not all, of its original brightness. My treatment will now be unblushingly academic. A few of the examples come from that source of wisdom, the *New English Dictionary*.

The term, then, has undergone two critical changes of meaning. The original sense, 'god-inspired', was already but faintly recalled at the end of the seventeenth century. Plato and the Greeks had used *entheos* of the divinely-frenzied poet or prophet, the passive channel of some message not his own which came down from heaven to the world. (The epithet 'god-intoxicated', applied to Spinoza, has a slightly different sense.) Again, our present usage was hardly current till late in the eighteenth century, though we find Joseph Warton's poem *The Enthusiast, or the Lover of Nature*, as early as 1740. The *New English Dictionary* defines the modern sense as 'rapturous intensity of feeling in favour of a person, principle, cause, &c.'; and tells us justly that the personal noun *enthusiast* has kept more visible traces of disparagement than has the abstract term or the epithet; as when we say, 'He is an enthusiast for the Baconian theory, or for casting horoscopes.' 'Enthusiasm for one's country' carries no such suggestion. For if we are told, 'He is an enthusiast for his country,' we answer, 'Well, why not?' However this may be, there is no doubt as to the intervening usage of the word. It was a slighting or damnatory one, and flourished long. Between the two Revolutions, it would startle us to find any one, not in irony or defiance, applying it to himself. It and its cognates are hostile terms. They are used by A, who does *not* think that B is divinely inspired or possessed at all, to express the fact that B falsely imagines himself to be so. Johnson, devout as he is, plainly approves the current use by his definition: 'a vain confidence of divine favour or communication'. Now who were A and B? Not to go too far back, we find Hobbes, in his *Leviathan* (i. xii, 1651), glancing with con-

tempt at the antique meaning of the word. Among
the 'superstitious ways of divination' he includes
'the insignificant speeches of madmen supposed to
be possessed with a divine spirit, which possession
they called enthusiasm'. A more surprising text
is found (*N.E.D.*) in that scholarly loyalist Henry
More the poet, a votary of the Christian Platonism
which has been resuscitated by Dean Inge. More,
in 1660, observes that 'if ever Christianity be exter-
minated, it will be by enthusiasm'. We know
what a Cavalier and churchman meant by that.
Dryden, in his *Absalom and Achitophel*, some twenty
years later, recites the rebel followers of Monmouth,
who include the Puritan citizens of London:

> A numerous host of dreaming saints succeed
> Of the true old enthusiastic breed;—

namely, of the ultra-Protestants, the parliamentarian
fanatics, members of any strange nonconforming
sect that might fancy itself to be guided by the inner
light. To Dryden such a net would be wide enough,
and would catch any one from Cromwell to Bunyan.
The reference, too, is often to the diction of the
'saints'—the diction of Cromwell's letters, or of
*Grace Abounding*, and of numberless devotees then
and since. We have the suggestive remark of
Swift, in his *Letter on the English Language*, that
'during the usurpation . . . an infusion of enthusiastic jargon prevailed'. But quotations from pure
men of letters need not be multiplied, as I shall
come presently to professed philosophers. The

bad sense is the regular one throughout our period. Gibbon, describing how the early Christians recovered from their first aversion to war and business, observes that

the human character, however it may be exalted or depressed by a temporary enthusiasm, will return, by degrees, to its proper and natural level. (*D. and F.*, ch. xv.)

The general tenor of the word is now clearer; and as to its lease of life, we may note that the bad sense survives, in corners, at least as late as 1829. It is found in that odd, bombastic, and forgotten book, Isaac Taylor's *Natural History of Enthusiasm*. Taylor understands by the term a disease of human nature, an affair of 'nosology', and a perversion of sober faith; a thing outlawed by both 'common sense and scriptural authority'. He quaintly cherishes the hope that it is 'not now justly chargeable upon any body of Christians'. He appears to mean all sorts of pietism and mysticism, and all assurance of personal contact with the divine. Taylor's language is emphatic but vague, and his whole point of view was already out of date. I return to the more formal treatment of the philosophers, taking texts from Locke, Hume, and Shaftesbury. Shaftesbury dates between Locke and Hume, but as he represents a compromise I will offer first the pure milk of the rationalistic word. I shall also quote John Wesley by the way.

IV

Locke, in 1690, analyses this distressing malady, which has raged so long. He is a physician; and the physician is in a threefold relation to the disease. First, he must not have it himself; next, he must try not to be, or not to show that he is, annoyed with it; and, lastly, he must study it, and throw out hints for cure or prevention. Locke fulfils all these conditions fairly well. 'Enthusiasm' occupies a chapter (xix, bk. iv), significantly placed, in his *Essay*. The preceding chapter is on 'Faith and Reason', and its drift is that reason, though it cannot provide, must nevertheless approve, and that it will approve, the data of faith; though Revelation is to be 'hearkened to' in matters where 'reason cannot judge, or but probably'. The succeeding chapter is on 'Wrong Assent, or Error'. Reason to Locke means the discovery and demonstration of real causes, in the world of nature and man, by valid methods. Wrong assent is given when the proofs do not suffice, or when there is a want of power or of will to deal with the evidence, or when probabilities or possibilities are taken as certainties. We may only assent to a proposition in proportion to the strength of the argument in its favour. This, no doubt, is the motto of all philosophers, but it is loudly emphasized by the British School. One form of wrong assent, or of belief founded on invalid evidence, is enthusiasm. To Locke, a convinced theist, the enthusiast seems to have taken an illegitimate short cut to the truth; which, if truth it be, can be rationally proved. Then he diagnoses the malady; he names no names, and may never have read his Bunyan; but the symptoms are for all the world like those of the 'chief of sinners'. Men, says Locke, persuade themselves that they are

under the peculiar guidance of heaven in their actions and opinions, especially in those of them which they cannot account for by the ordinary methods of knowledge, and principles of reason. Hence we see that in all ages men, in whom melancholy has mixed with devotion, or whose conceit of themselves has raised them into an opinion of a greate familiarity with God, and a nearer admittance to his favour, than is afforded to others, have often flattered themselves with the persuasion of an immediate intercourse with the Deity, and frequent communications from the Divine Spirit. . . . This I take to be properly enthusiasm, which, though founded neither on reason nor divine revelation, but rising from the conceits of a warmed or overweening brain, yet, where it once gets footing, &c. . . .

Then Locke, in his honest way, tries to fancy himself in the shoes of those deluded persons. His language might apply to George Fox, or to St. Teresa, or to Diogenes Teufelsdröckh. To them the light 'is clear and visible like the light of bright sunshine', and is its own proof. 'We may as naturally,' they say, 'take a glow-worm to assist us to discover the sun, as to examine the celestial ray by our dim candle, reason.' Then he turns and 'soberly' asks the enthusiast how he is sure that his revelation *is* a revelation, and proceeds:

The knowledge of any proposition coming into my mind,

I know not how, is not a perception that it is from God. . . .
Here it is that enthusiasm fails of the evidence it pretends
to. . . . Light, true light in the mind, is or can be nothing
else but the evidence of the truth of any proposition. . . .
To talk of any other light in the understanding, is to put
ourselves in the dark, or in the power of the Prince of Darkness, and by our own consent to give ourselves up to delusion,
to believe a lie.

Plainly there is no common ground between the
parties. We need not follow Locke's argument
further. He says in effect what most of the thinkers
of the Enlightenment were to say. But he differs
from the anti-clerical assailants that were to come.
A firm believer both in natural and revealed religion,
he rules out in advance the whole Wesleyan revival,
as well as its antecedents. Thus his piety separates
him from Hume, that true sceptic and unperturbed
observer, whose essay on *Superstition and Enthusiasm*
appeared about half a century after Locke's treatise.
And Hume differs, we shall see, in another important
way from Locke.

v

In reading Hume we feel we are in contact with
one of the strongest minds then at work in the world.
He dominates English thought in the mid-eight-
eenth century; most of its currents meet in Hume.
He is also one of its best writers; too much, I think,
has been made of his Gallic, and of his Scotch, idioms;
he is deceptively clear and easy to read; he is a
classical writer, in the good French meaning of the

term. But we must admit that when he comes to 'enthusiasm' his urbanity fails him, and Hume begins fairly to snarl:

> When this frenzy once takes place, which is the summit of enthusiasm, every whimsy is consecrated, human reason, and even morality, are rejected as fallacious guides ; and the fanatic madman delivers himself over blindly, and without reserve, to the supposed illapses of the spirit, and to inspiration from above. Hope, pride, presumption, a warm imagination, together with ignorance, are therefore the true sources of enthusiasm.

Such is Hume's judgement of the distinctive Protestant 'experience'. His repugnance is deep and full of alarm. All the more noteworthy is the reserve that he at once makes. One thing he hates worse than 'this frenzy', and that is 'superstition', by which he means Rome. And he adds, in order to be fair, that 'all enthusiasts have been free from the yoke of ecclesiastics'; that their fits, if violent, are soon spent; and they end, not by persecuting, but by falling into formalism and 'remissness and coolness in sacred matters'. In fact, 'superstition is an enemy to civil liberty, and enthusiasm a friend to it'. He points out how the 'Independents and Deists, though the most opposite in their religious principles, yet were united in their political ones, and were alike passionate for a commonwealth'; and how in France the Jansenists, as against the Jesuits, now, in 1741, 'preserve alive the small sparks of the love of liberty which are to be found in the French nation'. Part of this sketch we know

to be just.  Hume sees the historic alliance of the
Protestant with the popular party; and this, under
other names, was long to survive him.  Hume's
Toryism was not yet fully blown when he wrote the
passage.  He notes in his own way, as Locke fails
to do, that deep cleavage in the English people,
partly social, partly cultural, partly political, and
partly religious, which still persists.

We must not, however, simplify too much.  There
are all manner of cross-sections.  It is reason, not
in the philosophical meaning, but in the guise of
positive common sense, that sunders the typical
high churchman of the time like Samuel Johnson
from dissenter or evangelical and from their 'variety of
religious experience'.  Church and chapel, and also
sections within the church, faced each other over a
mental gulf.  One cause of this was the different up-
bringing of the parties.  It often was, and is, the inner
belief of the gentleman and scholar that 'enthusiasm'
was something uneducated; ill-bred, morbid, slightly
mad, and in no case essential to salvation.  It was
something that seethed and raved outside the great
caste; not a thing for gentry, nor for persons of
quality.  The enthusiast thus had a formidable team
against him: the rationalizing philosopher, the plain
educated man, the scholar and orthodox churchman,
and the man of the world or pagan fine gentleman.
This last personage might, like Lord Chesterfield,
be a nominal conformer, seeing that free-thinking
was equally ill-bred and absurd.  Perhaps the polar
extremes of the English temper in that age are seen

in Wesley and in Horace Walpole. Walpole went to hear and see Wesley, and was too clever not to admit his effectiveness. But the eternal word crops up once more; towards the end of his discourse, we learn, the preacher 'exalted his voice and acted very ugly enthusiasm'. Detachment could hardly go beyond this.

John Wesley was fully alive to the effects of such a prejudice. He was Oxford bred, scholarly, a master of terse pure English unadorned as well as of his peculiar professional eloquence. He was always eager to avert, to 'head off' as we say, the imputation of enthusiasm, and he used it himself, tactically, as a term of opprobrium. He applied it to mad and wild persons whose antics brought discredit on his message by their displays of false emotion and self-conceit. Such persons, he says,

think to attain the end [salvation] without the means . . . think themselves inspired by God, and are not. But false, imaginary inspiration is enthusiasm (1739).

Such was a man whom he found

riding through the town, hallooing and shouting and driving the people before him; telling them, God had told him he should be a King . . . I sent him home immediately to his work, and advised him to cry night and day to God, that he might be lowly in heart; lest Satan should again get an advantage over him [n]:

—a phrase, we note, oddly resembling Locke's own; and he adds that he 'was both surprised and grieved' at this 'genuine instance of enthusiasm' (1742). On another occasion Wesley turns round on those

who label *him* with the obnoxious word, and asks:
What, pray, might they mean by it? Do they
mean a believer in revelation?

Do you mean who maintains the antiquated doctrine of
the new birth, and of justification by faith? Then I am an
enthusiast. But if you mean anything else, either prove or
retract the charge (1761).

The person thus challenged by this admirable
politician might not care to deny the doctrine and
lose credit for orthodoxy.

VI

Let me return for a moment to the age of Anne
to show how the matter is regarded by another
philosopher. Shaftesbury, the third earl, is a
patrician of a different type to Walpole or Chesterfield. The pupil of Locke, in his *Characteristics* [n]
(1711) Shaftesbury shows himself in part Locke's
supporter; but his point of view is much wider.
Shaftesbury writes with a tedious elegance, rhetorically, and is soon overshadowed by stronger thinkers.
None the less, though in a strange way of his own,
he begins to announce the reaction against pure
logic and reason. The religious enthusiast, to begin
with, is not to be persecuted, but is to be cured by
a mixture of toleration and ridicule. The wise
Greeks and Romans smiled on every mania, and
there was no sectarian bloodshed then. Kill the
ailment, then, by 'good humour'; this is 'not only
the best Security against *Enthusiasm*, but the best

Foundation of *Piety* and true *Religion*'. Those who are thus treated will be fitted—so Shaftesbury puts it in his surprising style—for 'thinking with Freedom and Pleasantness on such a subject as GOD'; from our conception of whom we must expel all ideas of '*Stateliness* and *Moroseness*', while retaining those of '*Majesty* and *Greatness*'. As to the cure by ridicule, he has heard of a 'choice Droll or Puppet-Show at *Bart'lemy-Fair*', where the 'strange Voices and involuntary Agitations are admirably well acted, by the Motion of Wires, and Inspiration of Pipes'. This may be a legacy from Ben Jonson's old mockery, in *Bartholomew Fair*, of Zeal-of-the-Land Busy; who was probably, if we knew the heraldry of the case, a lineal ancestor of Mr. Pecksniff. Polite and benevolent patronage here goes to its extreme. In the same tone Shaftesbury pleads for the toleration of the Jews, and suggests that their real deficiency is in the sense of humour; they were 'naturally a very cloudy People, and wou'd endure little Raillery in anything . . . [their] sovereign Argument was, *Crucify, Crucify*'.

Shaftesbury afterwards expands these ideas. He adds that the modern, bastard variety of enthusiasm must be distinguished from the nobler Platonic application of the word; 'for Inspiration is a *real* Feeling of the Divine Presence, and Enthusiasm *a false one*'. And in *The Moralists* he breaks out in defence of the real thing. He now means by the term all kinds of lofty emotion, inspired by

208

oratory, music, patriotism, war, or learning; and
even, it appears, by mathematics, which do not
furnish, as he truly says, the pleasures of sense;—
by everything, in fact, *except* evangelical religion.
In a later work he says that there is 'a kind of
*Enchantment* or *Magick*' in the thing, and that it is
'a very natural *honest* Passion', having 'properly
nothing for its Object but what is *Good* and *Honest*'.
But it is apt to go astray, and he again deplores the
excitement of the zealots, who

curse, bless, sing, mourn, exult, tremble, caress, assassinate,
*inflict* and *suffer* MARTYRDOM, with a thousand other the
most vehement Efforts of variable and contrary Affection.

The atheist, too, is tarred with the same brush;
for have not Vanini and other fanatics faced the
pyre for *their* notions? Then Shaftesbury joins in
the usual chorus; he condemns the intolerance with
which superstition and enthusiasm have burdened
the earth; now on Papistical, now on Protestant
lips.

Shaftesbury, it is plain, has not got so far as Hume
in his analysis. He speaks of the ailment much as
a typical Whig noble of the last age or an old-
fashioned Oxford don might speak of the Salvation
Army, as a painful aberration, or at best as a perversion of something that might have been good.
At the same time, outside this region, Shaftesbury
said what no one else of his time said so distinctly.
He partly rescued the world from its ill associations,
though he was little thanked for doing so. He

spoke out, in his affected way, for the artistic feelings, and for more than the tempered and sensible
enjoyment of music and letters. His rhapsodies did
something in the age of Swift and Defoe to keep
alive the spirit of Plato; and herein he is an ally of
Berkeley. He sketched out a loose optimistic creed,
which the shrewd coarse assaults of Bernard de
Mandeville could not wholly demolish; and he set
his face against the barer rationalism of his age,
being himself, in his own sense of the term, a true
enthusiast.

## VII

The conflict here described is not merely a piece
of dead history; the combatants live on under other
names; they can perhaps never be reconciled, and
neither can ever extinguish the other. Those who
are favoured with the kind of experience which is
in dispute, seldom think that it needs or admits
of proof. They may build a logical stairway of
doctrine, or of discipline, up to a certain point;
but this, like some fabric of Piranesi's, breaks off
suddenly, and the next stride is into a precipice of
air. Sometimes, be it noted, those who have enjoyed
the experience, on mature reflection repudiate it as
a dream when one awaketh in the morning; but this
is not usual. On the other hand, the men who
analyse and verify to the bitter end are seldom,
in the nature of the case, the favoured ones. History
at any rate seems to show a great gulf fixed between

two permanent types of mind—between Locke and Bunyan, or Wesley and Gibbon. Only since those days the attitude of the analyst has changed. The enthusiast is now studied, with some sort of dramatic sympathy, in all his varieties, in order to see what fact in human nature may lie behind his distinctive experience. This change of temper is due not so much to the renewal of poetry and romance as to the scientific and historical spirit, which has brought all things under the category of Becoming and has tended, by that process, to swamp the question of truth or falsehood. In the theological world material causes have also been at work. Once outlawed, the Methodist and kindred movements came to be respectable and prosperous, founding thousands of chapels with millions of worshippers, and reacting powerfully on the established church. Their findings could no longer be dismissed or patronized, and the contributions of the 'free churches' to exegesis and theological scholarship have been immense.

I have tried to state this issue with equity, though of course only in outline; but it may be fairer to state, if need be, where my own sympathies lie. Art and poetry (which 'nothing affirmeth, and therefore never lieth') are not here in question, but intellectual conviction. I am, then, all for reason, and against 'enthusiasm'; but for reason in the following sense. The logical reason, of course, cannot furnish the full matter of experience; the affections, the moral emotions, and the mystical or religious vision, all contribute and put in their claim. Reason, as I see it, must at last decide the validity of that claim. At the worst, it must keep the position of a co-partner whose signature is requisite if the cheque is to be honoured. There are systems that seem to reason in favour of the cult of non-reason or unreason—a process that is like trying to blunt the knife with its own blade. It is said truly that reason itself is only a knife, or implement, evolved like the rest of the mind, and, in its explicit form, evolved later than the rest. But then it is evolved, after all, for self-defence; to check and judge, to approve or disapprove whatever seems to be asserted by the affective and visionary part of us. Science and reason, then, are trying to sift the question whether the 'enthusiast', in the widest sense of the term, is *right*. Whatever science says on such matters will always be disregarded by the body of mankind. But science itself goes on its way, disregarding the body of mankind. If I am asked what science *does* say on the point at issue, I reply that no one has discovered any test by which the point can be decided; and that the burden of a proof which shows no signs of being forthcoming, or of being put in intelligible or communicable terms, still rests on the shoulders of those who assert that the enthusiast reads his own experience aright. In this sense, then, if an amateur may make such a profession, I follow Locke and Gibbon, believing that their shades, like that of Julius Cæsar, are mighty yet.

# The Nature of Literary Criticism

It is a pleasure and a distinction to be called yet once more to lecture in the Owens College, and that upon the Ludwig Mond Foundation. My first appearance here was long ago—just within historical times; the last, when I gave one of the lectures established in memory of that learned and noble thinker, Robert Adamson. I must pass to my text, but shall mention other Manchester names that are held in great regard.

The word 'critic' to many people suggests something negative, not to say bloodless and barren. It is capable of rousing the lay mind much as the word 'expert' rouses the legal mind. As one of your own prophets, C. E. Montague, has said, the critic's plight is that of Falstaff: 'men of all sorts take a pride to gird at me'. The common term 'appreciator', again, smacks of the vintner's catalogue, and of pure connoisseurship; as though art were to be judged only by the mental palate, and not by the whole of our faculties. But instead of losing time, in defence of the critic's calling, let me define certain terms as I shall use them.

I cannot speak of music or the fine arts, but shall keep, throughout, to literature, not touching on the psychological basis or mutual connexions of the arts; but must owe in passing a salaam, and may more than once betray a debt to Professor Alexander's writings on art and on 'values'. Next, by literature I mean poetry; and shall use that term in its un-English sense of *Dichtung*—all imaginative invention be it in verse or prose; work that stands to be judged, first and last, as creative. Charles Lamb's *Dream-Children* and De Quincey's *Three Ladies of Sorrow* could in French be called *poèmes*. It might be awkward to speak of *Esmond* as a poem; still, it is *Dichtung*, and is to be judged simply as art. True, we can if we so choose judge Berkeley's dialogues or the *Decline and Fall* simply as art, for they are great compositions and to style and structure they owe much of their survival value; yet, since their first aim is to discover truth or advance knowledge, plainly such a judgement is insufficient. Works of this order are sometimes described as 'applied literature' in contrast with 'pure literature'; it is a rough distinction that up to a point will serve. Mr. Lascelles Abercrombie's[n] tractate on the *Principles of Literary Criticism* can be studied with much profit on this and on many a kindred question.

What, then, *is* the criticism of poetry, thus defined? Let me say first what I think it is not.   1. It is not

the *historical* study of the subject; neither is it the
body of *scholarship* devoted thereto; although
without these great allies it cannot travel far.   2.
Nor is it a *theory*; it is not that branch of Æsthetic
which is called Poetic; although Poetic and criticism
continually interpenetrate.   Every critic has *some*
philosophy, some poetic, be it only implicit; and not
least, when he disclaims all theory and avers that
he is simply wording his impressions.   For this too
is a creed, like all other forms of agnosticism.   3.
Nor is criticism a branch of *psychology*, though it
often draws upon psychology.   The most famous
proposition of the kind in the world is Aristotle's
account of the effect of tragedy in 'purging'—or
purging away—two of the moral emotions, fear and
pity.   Criticism is none of these things, for it is
*practical*; an art or craft like drawing; and all these
other kinds of knowledge may serve it as drawing
may be served by a knowledge of anatomy.   It is
also a *product*, like the poems which are its subject-
matter; and it may itself be an art-product, if the
critic, as so often has happened, is himself a poet or
has a poetic soul.   The product may itself be a
poem, though not in metre—a poem about a poem,
as when Charles Lamb [n] is speaking:

I never saw anything like this dirge except the ditty which
reminds Ferdinand of his drowned father in the *Tempest*.
As that is of the water, watery, so this is of the earth,
earthy.   Both have that intenseness of feeling which seems
to resolve itself into the elements which it contemplates.

The allusion is to John Webster's dirge,

> Call for the robin redbreast and the wren,
> Since o'er shady groves they hover,
> And with leaves and flowers do cover
> The friendless bodies of unburied men . . .

Lamb's few words contain all the essential elements of a critique. First, they are the expression of a vision peculiar to the speaker and unique in character. Next, he identifies himself with the poet's mood and vision. Then he interprets it, and retranslates it in poetic words that illuminate *our* vision. Finally he passes a judgement on the poem's rank and worth; for nothing less is implied in the comparison with Shakespeare. The ancient critics, and especially Aristotle, laid much emphasis on rank, on the hierarchies of poetic kinds and styles; they regarded some of these as superior in the order of nature to others, just as some species of animal, or of political constitution, were superior. I shall touch again on this issue; but meantime we must not go too fast. The more modern habit is to linger at the stage either of enjoying, or of interpreting and retranslating, and perhaps never to go further, never to face the question of ranks and of universal values at all; and even to assert, as remarked before, that these do not exist. But before discussing such questions let me remind you of some of the chief tribes and families of critic as they appear in history.

1. It is well known that three at least of the strongest intelligences on record have theorized, and that in a systematic fashion, upon poetry: these are Aristotle, Dante, and Hegel. Poetic has its niche in their fabric of philosophical thought. The chief thinker of our time who has made the same attempt is Benedetto Croce.[n]  2. Many creative minds of great eminence, mostly poets, have spoken, not indeed on system, but in flashes of wisdom, about their art and about fellow-poets. There is the deep voice of Goethe, musing aloud on Shakespeare and Byron, on Sterne and Goldsmith; and there is the voice, a golden voice, however fitful and broken, of Samuel Taylor Coleridge. A host of other English poets have illuminated criticism, from Sidney to Wordsworth and from Shelley to Matthew Arnold and Robert Bridges. Other nations, and above all France, can show a similar record.  3. Near to these come the poetic and apprehensive souls who do not use verse or use it only by the way; I have already quoted Lamb. In England the typical pure-blooded critic of this kind is William Hazlitt, the great enjoyer and discerner, to whom poetry and drama and the life of man and his own bitter-sweet memories and passions are all one thing, a single fund of experience, which it is his supreme solace to word, and to hear himself communicating.  4. But there is also the professional, the deeply instructed and flexible type of

critic, not primarily of poetic temper, who thinks of his craft chiefly as a clue to mental biography and the exploration of character. The greatest of this band is Sainte-Beuve, whose life overlaps that of the oldest amongst us. 'Ce que je fais, c'est de l'histoire naturelle littéraire.' Sainte-Beuve's works fill many shelves, and have worn well; they are always good to go back to, whenever we may fear that we are dropping into prejudice, or acridity, or commonplace. His artistic findings are also precious, and I shall quote him before concluding. There are many other kinds of critic—legislators like Boileau, prophetic rebels like William Blake. The tale is told, down to the year 1900, with a fullness and judgement so far unexcelled, in Saintsbury's *History of Criticism and Literary Taste in Europe* (1900–4). 5. Since then there have been developments, and I shall be quoting some of our younger writers. The school and influence of Croce have grown. I hear that the psycho-analysts, those surgeon-dentists of the soul, have applied their tools to poetry; but I must plead ignorance of their doings. In our own country, especially at Cambridge, a not unfruitful psychology, in the hands of Mr. I. A. Richards [n] and his friends, has sought to sharpen our sense of the poet's process and of his meaning and to warn us of the traps in the path. Richards has practised this method on the *corpora nobilia* of his own students with instructive results. But I am not affecting even to sketch the history of criticism. It is itself a matter for a long college course; and I am glad to think that such a course has been held, for nigh forty years without a break, in this university. It was approved at the outset by one of your greatest founders, Principal, later Sir Adolphus, Ward; it was conducted for many years by Charles Harold Herford, whose perceptions and understanding of literature ever matched his reading, and that, in its range, was European; and the tradition, I know, has been highly sustained by the present professor and by his colleagues, all specially versed in the critical field. The same course flourishes in some other English universities, and may be thought of as a descendant of the time-honoured Scottish curriculum on Rhetoric.

6. I am saying little of this great and indispensable army, which brings up the rear, of the scholar-critics: historians, editors, and expositors; with their alarming array of auxiliary sciences, linguistic, metrical, textual; with their task of leading their pupils, and the public, to the clearer enjoyment of poetry; and their more special one, in places of learning, of training a chosen band of 'researchers' and turning many admirable doctors of letters loose upon society. Croce,[n] you will say, is too hard upon our pursuits when he exclaims:

Is this enjoyment of poetry, this delight in beauty, rare or common? It is both: as a settled habit it is rare, reserved for select spirits who are born to it and trained by education; it is common, as the native tendency of ingenuous minds. The place where it is hardest to find is precisely among the professional students of poetry and of its historical achievements. They seem gifted with a strange immunity, which lets them all their life handle the books of the poets, edit and annotate them, discuss their various interpretations, investigate their sources, furnish them with biographical introductions, and all without suffering so much contagion as to experience in their own persons the poetic fever. After all, it is much the same in religion, which is felt by lofty minds and by the humble plebs, but not by those who handle the sacred vessels, by the priests and sacristans, who go through their ritual unconcerned, and sometimes with little reverence.

We too, at times, in school or college, may have thought that our pastors failed to make us feel the pleasures of poetry—how it is a Zion, a land of pure delight where saints immortal reign. A similar idea is expressed by a great scholar and editor, the late Dr. John Sampson,[n] who observes that

The intellectual elevation of the Literary Professor is sadly discounted when we reflect that the chief life-work of these venerable scholars is to appreciate and expound masterpieces reeled off in light-hearted moments by curly-locked striplings for their own amusement.

III

We may take these warnings to heart, and proceed. The work of the critic or teacher is to make poetry easier, and not harsher, to his hearers; all his interpreting must be judged by his success in that adventure. But why, after all, speak of critics as a class apart, when all mankind belong to it? Every one passes a judgement, which is partly a statement of impressions and partly an award of merit, on a story or a play, or even on a word. We begin in the nursery with an epithet—and many all their lives never get beyond that. 'This is good, or bad, or nice, or not nice, or delightful, or dreadful, or delightful in spite—or because?—of being dreadful';—and there, in the germ, is the central problem, perhaps still unsolved, of the pleasure that we take in tragedy. The adult elaborates these findings and seeks for reasons. But the elements of the process are always the same: a more or less passive reception of the poem; an effort to interpret it in the light of whatever knowledge of life, culture, and imagination we possess, and to seize the poet's intent and the measure in which it is realized; and lastly, an effort to answer Victor Hugo's question, 'L'œuvre est-il bon ou est-il mauvais?';—and, before answering, to ask what that question *means*.

This is but a working description, and I must leave the professional psychologist smiling at its crudeness. The elements which we may call receiving, understanding, and judging or ranking, need not occur in the mind in that fixed order. They are disentangled out of a confused act of apprehension that is more or less highly charged with feeling. Different minds, as I said, lay varying weight on one or other of them, perhaps to the disparagement of the rest. I will first say a word on some of the modes of receptive, sometimes called impressionistic, criticism; next, will try to describe the two chief principles of rating, or valuation, which have been in vogue, and which, it will be seen, are in conflict; and then, since it seems only fair not to shirk the question or to remain purely descriptive, will sketch my own notion of the critic's scope and business.

Croce is very severe, in the æsthetic as in the ethical field, upon the hedonist,[n] the man who judges poetry by the pleasure, the physical thrill, which it awakens in him. Art, he says, gives pleasure, but is not, in its essence, the pleasurable. Croce has read the Cambridge lecture in which the poet of the *Shropshire Lad* tells his learned audience of the sensations in his skin which assure him of the real presence of poetry. But we should not neglect such evidence. A late friend of mine, a great Dante scholar and not a sentimental person, I have seen in a public lecture strike his breast, in despair of conveying the appeal of the immortal passages, and exclaim, 'You feel it *there*.' An American poetess of note is reported as saying, 'If I feel physically as if the top of my head were taken off, I know this is poetry.' These are but versions, in rude physical terms, of an ancient doctrine. In Plato's *Ion* we hear how the poet or reciter is filled with a rapture that comes down from heaven as if through a magnetic chain, how it takes him out of himself, and the hearer likewise, who shares in the same *enthusiasm*; and how others, such as the under-masters of choruses, minister in their turn to the effect. Amongst these menials, no doubt, are our professors of poetry. Well, no one should talk of these matters who has never experienced such sensations. We are caught up by a phrase or a line and are moved to work outwards from it and to try to interpret it—there is no fear that the vision, if a true one, will vanish under analysis. Even quite young persons can be captured in this fashion. A boy can be moved by the dialogue of Cordelia with Lear. 'So young, and so untender?'—'So young, my lord, and true.' Often the simple, self-evident poetry is the greatest.

The words from *Lear* take us straight into the world of the pieties and the primary moral emotions; we scarcely think of them as words. But short of this it is possible to be in love with words for their own sake. Mr. Michael Roberts in his acute *Critique of Poetry* (1934) holds, I think too rigidly, that

literary criticism is a study of words, the effect of words on the reader, and the way in which the writer puts words together.

C. E. Montague was full of this passion, though his critical range of course far transcends it. Perhaps the intense contemplation of English sounds and syllables was made more familiar to us all by some sayings of Robert Louis Stevenson, and he may well have encouraged it in Montague,[n] who, in the posthumous book *A Writer's Notes on his Trade*, expresses it with a fervour that none of the poets, such as Miss Sitwell, who have spoken in the same sense, can well have bettered. We hear how the mind of 'a writer or a good reader' will finger single words and caress them, adoring the mellow fullness or granular hardness of their several sounds, the balance, undulation or trailing fall of their syllables, or the core of sunlike splendour in the broad, warm, central vowel of such a word as 'auroral'. Each word's evocative value or virtue, its individual power of touching springs in the mind and of initiating visions, becomes a treasure to revel in.

But that last sentence carries us outside the mere sound, into the realm of meaning and association. And this, in its turn, implies not only something that can be clearly stated to the reason—and there is always, in true poetry, that something—Rossetti's 'fundamental brainwork'—but also something not so to be captured, a vaporous bright penumbra of visions, eluding us like spots in the eye, which the critic can seldom, unless he too be a poet, word with any clearness. Of him too, in his lesser degree, as of the poet, Shelley's words are true, that 'the mind . . . is like a fading coal, which some invisible influence, like an inconstant wind, awakens to transitory brightness'.

## IV

But our quest to-night is something more definable, and I pass to the hardest part of my argument, which concerns the critic as *valuer*. If we are asking for philosophy, there is one radical problem which I must leave to the philosophers, having no sort of complete answer to it; and I can but suggest a possible line of approach. It is this: How, if ever, can we *escape* from our personal raptures, impressions, preferences, interpretations, findings, into any absolute judgements, or universal principles, which shall be good for all men? As an old poet says, 'Can man by no means creep out of himself?' How say, if we can say, that there is something comparable in art to the alleged permanence and objectivity of the moral law? How, again, say —and this is a different though allied question, that a certain *kind* of poetry, be it epic or lyric or drama, is intrinsically the 'highest'? Or, again, by what right can we say, that in the nature of the case, and in confirmation of the instinct of common sense, certain works like the *Iliad* are *inherently* greater than, say, *The Deserted Village*? or, in the words of the great critic—an 'appreciator' indeed —whom we call 'Longinus',[n] that

by a sort of natural impulse, we admire not the small streams useful and pellucid though they be, but the Nile, the Danube and the Rhine, and still more the ocean.

Let us recall the two chief canons of valuation that are most familiar.

The first has played a great part in history, and consists in judging a poem by its agreement or disagreement with certain acknowledged ancient models, or, what is nearly the same thing, with critical rules that have been partly founded on those models and have won prestige. To enlarge on this would be to relate much of the history of criticism for two or three centuries after the Renaissance; the birth, flourishing, and decay of what is called the classical, pseudo-classical, or neo-classical school; and also much of the history of poetry, which includes Milton's epics and his tragedy. For these are framed very largely upon ancient patterns and theories. Aristotle had laid down, partly from inspection of examples and partly on first principles, that a special type of tragedy—say the *Œdipus King*, was intrinsically the highest, alike in the structure of the plot, the moral make-up of the foremost figure, and the effect on the emotions of the spectator. This view had an immense influence on theory and practice; and it acquires more than an historic interest when we find that some of Shakespeare's tragedies happen to answer, although the poet was innocent of Aristotle, to the philosopher's definition of the leading figure, or hero:—one who is neither a monster nor perfect, but a man like ourselves, who is brought low by some flaw in his nature, or Achilles' heel. This is but one example. The last Englishman of note who sought to draw us back to Homer and Sophocles, and himself to write with these patterns well in mind, was Matthew Arnold. He made his chapter of an epic, *Sohrab and Rustum*. He threw out certain formulæ, based on his study of his models; as that all depends in poetry on the 'high seriousness' of the subject, or that poetry is a 'criticism of life'. The phrases have been much battered, and are too narrow, but I believe they are still of value and that the most valuable word in them, as I shall plead again, is the word *life*.

But the defect of this whole point of view is too familiar to dwell upon. New creative patterns, such as the romantic drama, are for ever forthcoming, and refuse to be judged by precedents or rules. The history of letters consists in such developments. These new patterns can be judged only by the event;—ah, and what is meant by saying that? Here I reach a more modern conception of poetic values, which does not depend on precedent or external rule at all. The test may be described as an *internal* one, furnished by the poem itself. The most thorough-going exponent of this view is Croce. The following sketch is much in debt to Croce, but is not offered as an exposition of his view, nor does it keep to his terminology. His Æsthetic is fitted into his intricate and comprehensive system of thought, to which a short summary could only do violence. The case for the 'internal' test is stated as it appears to myself.

v

The value of a poem is measured by the degree of harmony between the poet's *vision* and his *handiwork*—terms that I use for lack of better. Croce's word 'intuition' has other associations than those which he attaches to it; he appears to equate it with 'expression'—they are the same fact in different aspects. The familiar distinction between 'matter' and 'form' is full of traps. 'Matter', 'subject', and 'content' suggest only a *caput mortuum*—the poet's

227

vision and intent stript of just what makes them personal to himself. 'Form' suggests something that is on the surface, or all surface,—the verbal or metrical detail; or else, the bare bones of the poem, its arrangement and structure. 'Vision' is Blake's word, and seems more inclusive than any other. 'Handiwork' suggests both process and result: vision as realized in words.

The next question whether there be a specific 'æsthetic sense' is not debated here. But I should argue that if it exist it is present or latent in all men, from the savage who feels that his mate is comely, up to Michelangelo! that it is the same in essence whether its object is art or nature; and that it is we ourselves who read beauty into the face of nature (and, presumably, into each other's faces) by a process of selection that may be called artistic:— a contention that seems to be nearly that of Professor Alexander. In any case, the main principle is the 'autonomy of art'—'art for art's sake', but in a new sense; the independence, namely, of each single work of art,[n] which is subject only to the canon of harmony. In one passage Croce says that the sole critical question about a work of art, A, is whether it *is* a work of art or not. I should accept this saying, with an important addition to be stated presently.

The poem, then, is not to be judged by its moral elevation or moral meanness. Let the poet be as lofty as he will; his vision may well be morally inspired; but the question is, whether it has fully and perfectly realized itself in the handiwork of words.  Perfection, in art, means beauty or grandeur or both; I will assume this, without embarking on the radical problem of what those words mean; they are things undeniable, once we are in their presence.  Also I accept the idea, now becoming much more familiar, that the poet does not truly *know* what his vision is, or is to be, until the handiwork, at least in his own mind, is completed.  Its value then is defined by this entire accord; not by the moral worth, taken by itself, of the product; not by its place in the history of poetical topics or of the poetical instrument; nor by the philosophical truth of what is said, when this is rationalized into prose; and least of all by the pleasure (though this may be a *proof* of the harmony) which the work may give to any person or to any number of persons.

The issue, thanks in great measure to Croce, seems thus to be newly defined; and much lumber is swept away.  Yet there are problems, already mentioned, which this formula does not seem to solve.  The canon of inward harmony offers no direct answer to the inquiry, How (if at all) do we reach any universal values in the field of art?  What, again, is the meaning of the judgement of common sense that some species of poetry, and the masterpieces that represent them, are *inherently* higher, or greater, than other species, and than other products that are just as perfect of their kind?

But there are some lesser difficulties which the canon does appear to meet. (i) If all that is demanded is a harmony, a realization of the vision, what is the sense of saying that any subject—to take actual cases, a disease or the Sugar Cane—is 'beneath the dignity of art'? Such matters can be versified, at any rate with considerable finish. The answer is twofold. First, let us not beg the question, or rule out any product in advance, but let us judge by the product; or we may find ourselves forbidding Virgil to write upon crops and beehives. Secondly, if the product gives us no pleasure at all and is ugly or featureless, there is no breach of harmony, for there has been nothing to harmonize. Nothing whatever has happened, the work A is not a work of art at all but mere printed matter; and all zeros are equal. As Croce says, a work that is *wholly* ugly ceases even to be ugly, for it does not exist.

(ii) Another obvious doubt has to be faced, though it is not fatal to the theory. If goodness in a poem means harmony, then badness—or, when that is not an absolute term, imperfection— means some inner dissonance between vision and craftsmanship. Plainly the critic has to mark this —has, socially speaking, to warn others against taking the bad for the good or the worse for the better. New phases of poetry often begin with some such warning, be it just or not, against the forms and styles in vogue. Wordsworth attacked the nature-verse of the age of Pope on the score of its dullness of vision, which could not see the life of nature and dealt therefore in lifeless words.

Malherbe attacked what he thought the false handiwork of the school of Ronsard—certain turns and
figures and excesses of imagery—as violating the
genius of the French language. This was to pro-
claim a disharmony between the poet's intent, or
conception, and his product. Such attacks do their
work, and after a time their own excesses are
corrected; for Ronsard has long come into his own
again, and the youthful Pope is doing so at this
moment. (iii) One other caution, though needless,
may be added. In poetry, and to say it is no para-
dox, there may be a harmony *between* discords: in
this sense, that troubled, unresolved emotions in
the poet often demand an element of roughness—
which is only in a strained sense beautiful, for the
concept of grandeur or sublimity must also be
invoked here—in the words and rhythm. Shakespeare's *Coriolanus* and *Timon of Athens* are charged
with such effects: [n]

> What is here?
> Gold? yellow, precious, glittering gold? No, gods,
> I am no idle votarist: roots, you clear heavens!
> Thus much of this will make black white, foul fair,
> Wrong right, base noble, old young, coward valiant.

Here is plainly a kind of concord—what Mr. James
Sutherland, in his delicate little study *The Medium
of Poetry* (1934), calls the matching of the thought-
rhythm with the metrical pattern.

VI

This idea of an inner concord between the elements of a poem is nothing new, though it has been much elaborated in our time. I repeat the term *concord* because it is Dante's; and I know of no more compact and satisfying definition of the thing than one of his Latin sentences. He is stating the conditions of perfection for the species of lyric which he has decided to be the highest; and these are fulfilled when

the stateliness of the lines, as well as the lofty build of the sentences and the excellence of the single words, are all in concord with the weight of the thought or theme.[n]

That sentence contains not only the idea of harmony, but also, in full flower, the idea of values. Dante explains at length what he means by the *best* sort of words, of sentences, and of lines; and, above all, of *sententia*. Three themes fulfil the test: 'safety', or prowess in arms; love; and righteousness, or the direction of the will. Only these themes deserve, and only they evoke, perfect handiwork, which if bestowed on meaner themes is wasted and indeed is impossible. It is by this pathway, I suggest—though to pursue it would need a long discourse—that we begin to see the light and to escape outside the multiplicity of our personal judgements. We may agree that there are no absolute species of poetry, since new ones are always arising, and therefore that no rules based on existing species are absolute; and may also accept the canon of harmony between vision and handiwork as an essential *condition* of a perfect poem; so that it is the first business of the critic to consider this, i.e. to ask whether 'A' is a work of art or not. But not his last or only business. For Dante's words show the way out of the fatal circle of your opinion or mine into something more universal, namely into life itself—into the greater *concerns* and inspirations of poetry. To love and righteousness we could add the themes of death and nature. But the principle of harmony is taken to a higher plane by his remark that in chanting of these great concerns *only* the highest forms of expression are in place and suitable. Nor can we fairly limit these concerns by purely ethical terms, though they *include* the moral world; for the words love and nature take us further than that world.

Poetry, indeed, is not always on these severe heights; and there are perfections too in the valleys, or on the moderate plateaux. The critic must range over many altitudes and climates. I will now, if I may, sketch the vision that has often haunted my mind of the task of criticism. There is nothing new about it, and it leads up to a commonplace; but I beg indulgence if I seem to start too far from the subject.

VII

Imagine two great worlds, or seas, indefinite in extent and duration; one without us, and one within.

The first is the total of natural beauty and grandeur; qualities of which it is debated whether they reside in nature or only in our minds, but which in any case are only potential until they are contemplated and which can all be conceived of as matter for contemplation. The other is the total of man's inner life; of his impressions, passions, aspirations, ideas, dreams and dramas; for all dramas are ultimately spiritual. Every moving drop in that stream of life has its effect, and, in that sense, it never dies. The impressions of outer nature form part of this total. And yet all but an infinitesimal fragment of these units of experience loses its identity and is forgotten, melting into the next moment of the stream. Of that fragment, the identity may be preserved in outward shape, and possibly in memory. It is made by the poor minority of men, to whom it comes as a vision, and who try to catch and embody it in line, in colour, in marble and stone, in music, or in words. Some of these efforts succeed, and some of those which succeed are remembered. A good poem has the chance of lasting, though it may be for ever buried in a papyrus, or lost for a long time like our Old English verse. The language of *Beowulf* was for centuries forgotten. Or changes of taste or periods of mental blankness may have the same effect. But the poem—that unique expression of one man's charmed or impassioned or enlightened vision— *may* last, and be known and understood. You see that I have but come back to the ancient text of the immortality of verse. Art indeed is not every-thing, for science and philosophy are also among the powers that redeem mankind; but art alone has the quality that, apart from physical risks, its products retain their identity to the mind and senses, and so may abide.

The critic has his part in this preservative process. He may seldom find a treasure like FitzGerald's *Omar* or the medieval *Alisoun* or the songs un-earthed by A. H. Bullen. His usual task is one of rediscovery and interpretation like that of De Selincourt editing the *Prelude* or of Grierson editing John Donne. Sometimes he may be a poet himself. It was Swinburne who made it impossible any longer to slight the precious lyrical gift of William Collins and who first illuminated the poetry of William Blake. The history of poetry and of criticism is largely made up of such doings.

The ideal of the critic's craft now begins to define itself. I hope, more plainly. There is no need to claim too much for it. The poems that speak to all men need no professional certificate: the finding of *orbis terrarum* settles the matter. Audiences will for ever watch Hamlet and Falstaff; and here the best critic is the player; he comes nearer to the poet than the writer can ever do. A lyric like Gray's *Elegy* endures, and nothing we say about it makes much difference to its tenure. A perfect and impassioned love-song, say one by Burns, may speak to any enthusiast, any youth; so that Dr. Sampson's 'curly stripling', who made

the rhymes, is now re-embodied in the kind of
hearer for whom they were intended; and the
'venerable' writing man, coming between, is an
intruder and may well beat a retreat. For all this,
he has his uses. He is a rescuer, and his work is
to *elicit*: to mirror as truly as he can the poet's
vision, and to judge of its realization in the handiwork. For one thing, he is there to speak out. If
popular or consecrated poetry seems to him not
worth its fame, he is to say so, careless whether
posterity will reverse or deride his finding. As
Mr. Richards observes, 'far more of the great art
of the past is obsolete than certain critics pretend'.
The still living power of Johnson as a critic is due
to this kind of independence; as when he tells us
of *Paradise Lost* that

the want of human interest is always felt. . . . None ever
wished it longer than it is. Its perusal is a duty rather than
a pleasure.[n]

It is not true; but who would wish Johnson's
mistakes unsaid? It is easier to discount his prejudice than to imitate his honesty. The ideal critic,
no doubt, is without prejudice. Whilst at his easel
he must be deflected by no passions of his own,
political or religious; let him keep them for other
hours! In matters of art and thought, he is neither
church nor anti-church, neither for nor against
the national enemy, neither antinomian nor puritan.
Nor does he sit aloft, on a pedestal; for he tries to
enter, so far as he may, into the heart of his poet

and to re-collect—not 'in tranquillity'—*his* 'emotion'.
His material is thus the material of poetry itself;
and this (to quote a forgotten sentence) is

anything in the kingdoms of nature or of man, or in the
conception or legend of God, that can delight or hold the
imagination, or can intelligently trouble it; may indeed be
almost anything that with good reason leaves our mortality
still endurable and valuable.

### VIII

But to come down from these abstractions to the
historical scene of letters. The critic, even if he
keeps simply to the shining figures, has enough to
busy him for twenty lifetimes. It is almost enough
for him to try to define once more the virtue of the
*classics*. Here, in conclusion, I fall back upon
Sainte-Beuve and on his notable vision of a Temple
of Fame.[n] He is thinking of the natural families
of writers, and of the masters in each family. In
one corner, or shrine, he sees the epic poets of the
East; near them are the sages who have coined *la
morale humaine*, the higher wisdom, into maxims;
'the Hesiods, the Jobs, the Solomons,—and why
not Confucius himself?' In another space sit the
eternal charmers, led by Virgil—Virgil as modest
and as brilliant as on the day when he is said to
have recited his verse in public, and the Roman
theatre rose to salute him. Tibullus and Proper-
tius are of this company; and so, adds the French
critic, is Fénelon. On a hill near by are the Attic
masters of prose, easy, persuasive and exquisitely

simple; at their head stands Addison. In the centre are the three mighty ones, Plato, Sophocles, Demosthenes, 'whose names have become the ideal of art'. Not far away are the painters of life and manners, led by Cervantes and Molière; and on a height apart, Lucretius would be fain to debate with Milton 'the origin of the world and the disentangling of chaos' . . . There is more; but each of us can people the Temple as he chooses, and be rewarded if he can give his days to a single master.

Sainte-Beuve's dream can be found in his *causerie* entitled *Qu'est-ce qu'un classique?* and I will end with his account of what he means by the term:

This is how I would like to hear a true *classic* defined:— He is an author who has enriched the human mind, and has truly added to its treasury; who has brought it a step forward; who has found out some unequivocal moral truth; or has recaptured some eternal passion in the heart, where, as it seemed, there was nothing left to explore or know; —who has expressed whatever he has thought, or noted, or invented, in any form whatever;—but it must have width and greatness, it must be delicate, and full of good sense, and sane, and beautiful in itself. He is one who has spoken to all men, but in a style that is at once his own style and every man's—a style that is fresh, but without coinages (*néologisme*);—is both new and old, and is in every age without any trouble, a contemporary style.

Nothing can be more generous than this, or better framed to make the humblest critic think more highly of his calling; and also, like Malvolio, to 'think nobly of the soul'.

# George Saintsbury

Living on to eighty-seven, George Saintsbury found some compensation for the burden of years in the honours that he received and enjoyed. What he called, echoing the phrase of Gibbon, the 'browner shades', were brightened, perhaps unexpectedly. There was a kind of *renouveau* of his reputation. Mr. Nicholson's portrait in the Merton Common Room shows him well: the kindly, sagacious, and expressive eyes, under the skull-cap, and the lined features full of humane experience. There he sat in his room in Bath, facing one of the great city prospects of England; more and more house-bound, but reading and writing insatiably while his sight permitted; answering letters more briefly than of old, but always vivaciously, and always, as his habit was, by return; warmly regarded, both by the older and the younger sort: an institution now and almost a piece of history, but in heart and wit permanently young. Some years back, walking in the street, he had been knocked down by a taxi. He rose and spoke words to the cabman, who retorted that he ought to thank God for escaping with his life. 'I do thank God', was the reply

(which found its way into print), 'but I damn *you*':
a sentence that consoled Saintsbury for his bruises.
The *renouveau*, perhaps, was due in part to the
*Notes on a Cellar-Book* (1920), with their Bacchic
lore and their appeal to the world of judicious
feasters. They carried Saintsbury's name far beyond the literary class; a formal retort from those
whom he reviled as 'pussyfoots' would have delighted
him, but never came.

Later still appeared the three small square *Scrap-
Books* (1922–4), which are a mirror of the real, the
ultimate Saintsbury. The much-abused 'style' is
there, at its best and worst and freshest: whims,
jests, funny ferocities, sudden far-off allusions in
parenthesis ('divine Parenthesis', I think he once
called it), capitals, italics, rare or not rare quotations.
Everywhere a Sterne-like oddness and twist of
language—only it is not, like Sterne's, the effect of
care and artifice. It is the native idiom of the
speaker in his talk and letters and his thoughts.
Many who had disliked it were reconciled, once
they came to know and like the man. In his
writings he would bring in his ego, perhaps to
excess; but that mattered little if the ego attracted
you. To all those who censured the style, and to
numerous other bruisers, Saintsbury's answer was
that which he gave to the cabman. I make these
notes, after a friendship that began a generation ago.
I met him first when he came to examine with us
(most shrewdly and punctually he did such business)
at Owens College. At first, be it owned, he seemed

strange. He spent some time in expatiating on the enormities of a critic who had suggested that he, Saintsbury, did not know his Horace. The villain disposed of, he proceeded, after deciding, in the restaurant, that cold beef was the safest diet, to talk happily of many things; I forget what, but they might range from cheese to Charles d'Orléans, or from prosody to Pigott, the forger of the 'Parnell Letters', from whom he had once saved, as he was fond of relating, the old *Saturday Review*. This is part of the entertainment offered by the *Scrap-Books*.

I am not sure that the press notices have done justice to him as a critic and man of letters. The public, and even the reviewers, have been apt to salute with open mouth his learning and reading and to forget his brains. The learning, the *omnilegence*, were no doubt exceptional. 'Reading', he said, 'is to me like *mental breathing*.' And naturally, if you go on for seventy years reading very hard, and, like Macaulay, very fast, the sum mounts up. But we may easily make too much of that: there are plenty of pundits with full heads. The question is, what comes out of the heads; and Saintsbury's performance can hardly be judged without regard to what our American friends like to call the 'background': the setting of convictions, of sympathies and antipathies, within which his critical spirit found such free play. Now, if there is a single seat of honour, among those who discourse of Church and State, that is *beyond* the extreme Right, there, surely, sits Saintsbury. He must have been nearly the last of his clan. There are other high Tories, and Puseyites, greatly to be esteemed; but *he* gave in at no single point, in politics or creed, to what is called the modern spirit. The average Conservative probably smiled in approval, but 'thought that he could hardly go quite so far'. Saintsbury, in these matters, was a thoroughgoing Manichæan and proclaims it on every page. He comes out, sometimes in surprising places, with amazing and most amusing flings at the enemy; and only sourness could take offence. He was on the best of terms with many in the other camp, and it was a point of honour with him that opinions should not interfere with friendship. Only, he much preferred that such friends should have no half-convictions. 'So-and-so', he said once, 'is a good fellow, a brilliant fellow; I like him—but he has no *tie-beam*.' Some topics, naturally, did not come up in conversation; his uniform, like that of a most intelligent *abbé*, could only command respect. There was all the world of letters, and a good deal of life, left to talk about.

This Toryism was an admirable soil for a critic of Saintsbury's cast. For here, too, a similar point of honour ruled and, save for some inevitable small eruptions, he observed it nobly. His canon was simple: Keep your critical conscience clean, your artistic impressions and perceptions undistorted. Your author's opinions, his ideas in the abstract, are not your affair *while* you are talking of his art. 'L'œuvre est-il bon ou est-il mauvais?' and how, and why? You may abominate 'free love', and yet enjoy *Epipsychidion;* nay, you will catch its flying essence all the better for having conscientiously shelved its doctrine. No doubt Tom Paine was a wretch, but you will have a good word for his prose. This attitude is a source of strength to Saintsbury, since it sets no limit to his liking for whatever may be good; it makes for catholicity. He often defends it; the living work of art—that, he says, is the sacred thing for the critic. Not bare form, or mechanism, will be his quest, but perfect, and passionate or delicate, or at least sound, expression. Walter Pater long ago, as Saintsbury knew, had gently noted in him a certain over-emphasis on pure 'form'. And it is true, I shall suggest presently, that Saintsbury's books on metre and rhythm are the last word and logical outcome of his concern for form. It is also true (not to vex this ancient question further) that to sever the form from the 'substance' and 'ideas' is hardly possible; for where do these stop? The thing can be done, up to a point, but only for the purpose of analysis. Yet Saintsbury was far away from the queer mental taint of the so-called, and now, I suppose, all but extinct 'æsthetic' school. He sometimes, unjustly to himself, lays himself open, with his metaphors from 'vintages' and the like, to the charge of being a literary eqicurean. But he was not consistent here, for no one can be. His beloved classical poet seems to have been Lucretius, who moved him deeply, and that not simply as a poet and executant, but through his stern presentment of the human lot.

In Saintsbury there was a streak of what may be called conditional pessimism. He responded also to the Preacher; and he seems to say, 'That is what life looks like, what it really would be, *but* for all that I, so immutably, believe.' He had much depth, and even fierceness, of temperament, and responded no less to the *Song of Songs*. Yet he was far too big, too healthy, too full of Homer and Rabelais and Fielding, and too well versed in history, to rest there, or to inhabit any foolish 'ivory tower' of 'art'. Such freedom of mind, I repeat, is no bad foundation for criticism. Saintsbury, in any case, was born to urge and to apply his peculiar point of view; not that—an equally important one— of Professor Bradley; and still less that of Coleridge, whom he justly held to be one of the greatest of critics, and who cares, as we know, most unmistakably, for 'ideas' and 'substance'.

Another of Saintsbury's 'neglected First Laws of Criticism' is sound enough. As he puts it, 'B is not bad because it is not A, however good A may be'. Probably he has applied his canon to more authors, old and new, ancient and native and foreign, than any critic in the language. There is no man, however well informed, however unsympathetic, who cannot learn from Saintsbury; who cannot acquire from him not only new facts, but illumination. But before touching on his performance I ought to give a word to the devil's advocates. The volumes that fill so many shelves doubtless offer a large exposed surface to the censor. Writing so much and so fast (and the long years of journalism made composition too easy), Saintsbury could hardly be invulnerable. Far back in the eighties he was twice noisily assailed, first by Edmond Scherer and then by John Churton Collins, for some errors of detail in his literary histories. The censures were not all fair or well founded. Saintsbury hardly referred to them, but silently, in following editions, made the needful corrections. He was not at his best as an editor of texts, and more than once he passed errors of transcription. But these things must be seen in proportion; no English critic has covered so big a field of literature; and, in my belief (formed after seeing reams of his proof sheets) he was, on the whole, a very accurate chronicler, and made fewer mistakes than most historians who write on the grand scale.

Often, no doubt, he is too copious; and he suffers from a certain want of finality—not, indeed, in his critical judgements, which he seldom or never retracts, but in his expression of them. He will talk, again and again, of the same author, with unabated freshness, and without ever taming his language, and yet without decisively *stamping* it. So in the case of Tennyson, or Fielding, or Thackeray (of whom he is one of the extreme votaries). But most criticism is so tender a plant, fading in a night —unless it be that of Dante or Longinus—that it will hardly bear such treatment. Among Saintsbury's briefer works, indeed, can be found many shapely and delightful *causeries*, where this uncertainty does not arise. The best, perhaps, are in the three volumes of *Collected Essays and Papers, 1875–1920*, reissued in 1923–4. There are more than sixty of them, and many read as if written yesterday. Many deal with writers, Hood and Leigh Hunt, Lockhart and Jeffrey, on whom some dust has begun to settle. Others, like those on Praed or Peacock or Borrow, centre on some rare delightful gift or idiosyncrasy of a minor classic. Others are on Landor, Dickens, and the major authors of the last century. A few are on Dante, Shakespeare, Milton, but in each case with the significant addition—'and the grand style'. Nearly all show Saintsbury's skill in the craft of the *causerie* and are full of the 'minute sparkle' which he somewhere attributes to Sainte-Beuve. With these volumes I would rank the prefaces to the editions of Sterne and Fielding and Smollett and Peacock. All this can be read with pleasure by educated persons who are not students by profession.

None of Saintsbury's bigger books are more original and learned, or done with greater relish, than the *History of English Prosody* (1906–10) and the *History of English Prose Rhythm* (1912). The people who are truly enthusiastic over these topics could be gathered in quite a small dinner-party. Most men will echo Walter Raleigh:

> The spondee, dactyl, trochee, anapaest,
> Do not inflame my passions in the least.

But they do inflame the passions of the metrists, hardly two of whom agree, because, though they all *like* much the same things, they all *hear* them differently. Some of them raged when Saintsbury waved aside all disputes as to the physiological, or musical, basis of metre, and when he styled these questions '*meta*prosodic' or '*meta*critical'; meaning by '*meta*' that which lies too far behind the subject and is irrelevant. Certainly his own 'first principles', as to accent, quantity, and the like, are none too lucid; but this matters little to the result. His notation suffices for his purpose, which is that of the historian, enjoyer, and connoisseur. So he writes of Tennyson's *Dying Swan:*

> The poet takes the old equivalenced octosyllable of the thirteenth century and of *Christabel,* moulding it into an irregular stanza with more or fewer recurrences of rhyme as he pleases. But in the first of these stanzas he avails himself very little of anapaestic substitution. There are only two anapaests in ten lines. . . . In the third we come to the death-song itself, and the metre lengthens, unrolls, is transformed by more and more infusion of the trisyllabic foot, till the actual equivalent of the 'eddying song', the 'awful jubilant voice', the 'music strange and manifold', is attained. Such command of sound, joined to such power of painting, might, one would think, have sent good wits and good lovers raving. Yet Mill says nothing about it in the dawn, and George Brimley, when noon was drawing on, thinks it 'uninteresting' because there is no apron-string or medicine-bottle about it as in the *Gardener's Daughter* and the *May Queen.* . . .

Here, indeed, is 'gusto'; and there is much of George Saintsbury in those few lines. The book on prose rhythm, on which I must not dilate, is still more original, because the ground had hardly been broken before. The three-volume *History of Literary Criticism and Literary Taste in Europe* (1900–4) is his widest and lengthiest contribution to learning; it is, indeed, on the lengthy side. It has had many critics; but no one has tried to do the work again. Here, once more, the theoretical basis is not Saintsbury's concern; and Croce, I believe, has protested against the omission. Criticism is a branch of æsthetics, and æsthetics of general philosophy. Saintsbury's attitude, for which he argues with spirit, is not so easy to maintain while reviewing Aristotle or Lessing. Also, as W. P. Ker once noted, the treatment takes us 'some way from literature'. What do *you* think of what Saintsbury thinks of what Boileau thinks of what Longinus thinks of the Sublime? But then this treatment is in the nature of the work, unavoidable if a history is to be made at all. Saintsbury begins, not with theory, but with the books. He goes through the whole huge chronicle, including many a writer forgotten or obscure, expounding, documenting, annotating, swashing right and left, joking for light relief in the middle of a solemn argument, and enjoying all with unslackening energy. The later volumes, in my own opinion, are the best; but all are of value. Saintsbury's first principle is very much that of the writer who is known as 'Longinus'. He seeks, above all, for the transporting thrill of style and rhythm, caused by the passion of the artist behind them; the moment of electric contact between conception and expression. And surely, whatever more we may ask of literature, this at least is necessary.

I must ignore here the ample volumes on the French novel, the shorter ones on French and English literature, the mass of articles in the *Britannica* and in the *Cambridge History of English Literature* and much besides. No one can have read all Saintsbury's signed writings; and the unsigned ones, innumerable, are out of reach. And he said (the remark opens a vista) that he had, as a journalist, 'written almost as much on politics as on literature'. Once, at a dinner given to him in Liverpool, I was moved to quote the familiar *Quæ regio in terris?* and to say that wherever one wandered in literature, English or French or medieval Latin, Saintsbury was likely to have been there first. This is the bare truth, and it would be true of men more learned than myself. His acknowledged works certainly deserve a careful bibliography: it is a task for one of the many pupils whom he inspired and taught. There is room, too, for an anthology of his best pages. Time will surely pay its meed to a critic of so true a gift, of so high a rank, so animated, so single-minded, and so wide and just in his perceptions.

## James Fitzmaurice-Kelly

The literary and historical work of this illustrious scholar will be reviewed [n] by those qualified to judge it; I am no Spanish scholar, and I do but offer some record, and some impressions, of the man. Our acquaintance only began when Fitzmaurice-Kelly arrived in Liverpool in 1909; and he was one who rarely spoke about himself; so that these memories must be combined with evidence supplied on the best authority by others. It is right specially to acknowledge the contributions and suggestions of his intimate friend, of more than a quarter of a century's standing, Sir Edmund Gosse, the poet and critic; of Professor Wyld, now of Oxford, and formerly Fitzmaurice-Kelly's housemate in Liverpool; and, above all, of Mrs. Fitzmaurice-Kelly, who has furnished the greater part of the material.

James Fitzmaurice-Kelly was three parts Irish; his grandmother on the maternal side was French. Perhaps the reserve, which was so marked a trait in his character, was Irish; it was in any case accompanied, as in many of his countrymen, with much easy sociability and wit. His family was

Catholic. Menéndez y Pelayo [n] has observed that this fact, together with his nationality, freed Fitzmaurice-Kelly from many a British prejudice, and qualified him to understand the peculiar genius of another race and civilization. James was born on 20 June, 1857, at Glasgow, where his father, Colonel Kelly Bey, of His Majesty's Fortieth Foot, and at one time in the Egyptian Police, was then stationed. Colonel Kelly was called to India; and there the child went with his parents; but, at the age of nine, was sent home. James never again saw his mother; she died abroad; but he cherished her memory, and in later life prefixed her maiden surname, Fitzmaurice, to his own, as though to link it with any credit that he might win. He was put to school at St. Charles's College, Kensington; and with this institution he was to remain, for long after his boyhood, in close and affectionate relationship. Meantime, it was planned that he should enter the priesthood; but, on reaching the age of reflection, he abandoned this idea for good. The reading of Pascal influenced this decision, and it is not the first time that Pascal has failed to fortify the believer. But it is sufficient to say that he had 'no vocation'. Fitzmaurice-Kelly, whatever his ultimate convictions, remained in undisturbed relations with many Catholics and retained a keen sense of *l'esprit catholique*. He had many memories of Manning, with whom his family had been intimate. I have his copy of Wilfrid Ward's *Life of Newman*, an author of whom he often talked with zest. He appeared, however, always to care more for art, letters, history, and humanity, than for abstract thinking, and to have an essentially undogmatic mind.

The Church being thus excluded, another calling had to be chosen; but the choice was far from clear. Colonel Kelly's anxiety was natural; and, to please his father, James now embarked on the study of medicine. But this he did not carry far; again, he had no vocation. It could not be foreseen that he would be a great scholar; but he was clearly shaping, in some fashion, for a man of letters. We have not many glimpses of his youth. We know, however, that he had a musical gift of no mean order, and he trolled, like many another lad, the tunes of Gilbert and Sullivan's operas in a charming light barytone voice. In later life, too, he would delight his friends (if there were few enough of them present) by singing them from memory; and he could also chant many a song from French and Italian opera, and from Handel, and parts of Masses; and also— at the other extreme—English popular songs, even those of the music-hall, with all their 'patter'. The decision to give his life to the study of Spanish letters must have been formed during the eighties. It seems that for a time Fitzmaurice-Kelly inclined, instead, to Scandinavian studies; and, in fact, he came to acquire a close knowledge of Swedish. In the eighties, both Peninsular and Scandinavian literature were comparatively little studied in Britain; and Fitzmaurice-Kelly was always attracted by the 'lonely furrow', or, as he put it, by 'the undisturbed possession of a little plot of my own'. But he had already picked up some Spanish from certain school-fellows; even to the point, it is said, of reading *Don Quixote* in the original at a tender age. In 1885 we find him in Spain. He went there as tutor to Don Ventura Misa, the only child of the Count of Byona, in Jerez de la Frontera; and this pupil he helped through a legal examination. During this brief stay in the country Fitzmaurice-Kelly learned much more Spanish, and struck some roots, forming friendships with Juan Valera and Núñez de Arce amongst others. We may suppose that he came home with his devotion to things Spanish now assured.

Fitzmaurice-Kelly now threw himself upon litera-ture, scholarship, and journalism. A living was not very easy to make. He had not been through the collegiate mill and had no academic distinctions to show. Little is heard of him for some years. But he was soon a reviewer for journals of standing like the *Spectator, Athenæum,* and *Pall Mall Gazette.* He became known as an authority on Spanish subjects. He had also been taught by his mother to speak and write French with unusual purity and ease. Fitzmaurice-Kelly was notably assisted and encouraged by the poet, essayist, and journalist, William Ernest Henley, to whom he acknowledged, in his own words, 'a vast intellectual debt'. The influence of Henley is known to those who remember or study our annals at the end of the century. He had his share of genius, and gathered a band of young men around him, in whom he kindled a passion for letters. He made them write, found them work, stamped his own manner, with its eloquence and *emphase*, upon them, and often instilled into them a strange kind of boisterous, literary Toryism. Fitzmaurice-Kelly was proof, I think, against both the Toryism and the manner. He was a keen Liberal and a fervent admirer of Gladstone. His own style, naturally limpid and delicate, must not be judged from the prefaces that he contributed to the seventeenth-century translations, reprinted by Henley, of the *Celestina* (1894) and of *Don Quixote* (1917); for these prefaces were much overlaid by the additions of the editor, who took a masterful view of his duties. But the taste and exact scholarship of Fitzmaurice-Kelly are there. Meantime he had produced in 1892 *The Life of Miguel de Cervantes Saavedra*, which was to be wholly rewritten twenty years afterwards in the light of later discoveries. A much more important venture was the *History of Spanish Literature* (1898). Sir Edmund Gosse, the editor of the series in which the book appeared, prevailed slowly and with some trouble upon the diffidence of the author. When at last it appeared, it was applauded by Henley with due vigour; 'you *have* come off', he cried, 'and no mistake; by God, I'm proud of you!' But the book was also praised on authority, and founded Fitzmaurice-Kelly's wider reputation. It has been appraised by the experts, and I must not trespass; but I am moved

to quote some sentences of Menéndez y Pelayo,[n]
which are found in his long prologue to the
Spanish translation, in the midst of many suggestions and criticisms:

Fitzmaurice-Kelly no es un árido erudito, sino un fino y
delicado literato, un hombre de gusto y de alma poética, que
siente con viveza lo bello y lo original, y expresa con elegancia
y hasta con calor su entusiasmo estético. Aun en los límites
de un compendio logra evitar la sequedad y se hace leer
con agrado. Versado en todas las literaturas modernas, y
muy especialmente en la francesa y en la de su país, ameniza
su trabajo con curiosas comparaciones, con reminiscencias
familiares á los lectores británicos, y traza indirectamente,
á la vez que la historia de la literatura española, la de su
influencia en Europa y sus relaciones con las demás literaturas, ofreciendo en est punto novedad, singularmente para
los españoles.

We need not try to better this description, which
supplies a corrective to a few of our journalists who
found Fitzmaurice-Kelly so learned that they could
only perceive his learning. The qualities thus
noted by Menéndez y Pelayo in 1901 were to mark
all that Fitzmaurice-Kelly wrote afterwards.

He now became much better known. Mrs.
Fitzmaurice-Kelly's bibliography dispenses me from
attempting to chronicle his writings. Some of these
were at first lectures, and as a lecturer Fitzmaurice-
Kelly came to be much in request. He gave
Taylorian lectures at Oxford and MacColl lectures
at Cambridge. In 1907 he toured round many of
the chief American universities with success, though
not without fatigue. He was honourably received;

Columbia made him a Doctor of Letters, his first and only distinction of that kind. He was, as I have noted, self-trained, and may have been all the more put upon his mettle to show that he could be as rigorous and thorough, and as merciless to himself, as the most finished product of the older universities. 'Fué lector impertérrito', said Sr. Sanín Cano justly in the *Nación* of Buenos Aires, writing in December 1923. This generous and just article I shall quote again. Fitzmaurice-Kelly's conscience as a scholar is evident even to the layman, and is but one side of the probity, moral and intellectual, which pervaded his character. In Spain, meantime, he received recognition and title. As the representative of England he attended the Cervantes tercentenary of 1905, and he was made a Knight of the Order of Alfonso XII.[1] But he still had no fixed installation, and had to live largely by lectures and his pen. He wrote many articles of importance for the *Encyclopædia Britannica* (eleventh edition); and some of them, which fall outside Peninsular studies, show his historic instinct and his wide outlook on the field of literature. One phrase, 'the desire for the one just form, which always inspires

[1] Other honours: C. de las R. R. Academias Española (1895), de la Historia (1912) y de la de Buenas Letras, Barcelona (1914); C. da Academia das Sciencias de Lisboa (1922); Member of the Advisory Board of the Hispanic Society of America (1904); Fellow of the British Academy (1906); Member of the Athenæum Club, London (1920); Examiner to Civil Service Commissioners, for Oxford Honours School, Cambridge Tripos, etc.

the literary artist', gives a clue to his own ideal as a writer. The remarkable pages on 'Translation' may be named; and those on 'Maupassant' well show Fitzmaurice-Kelly's gift of criticism in miniature. 'Tuvo', says Sr. Sanín Cano, 'por la forma una pasión intolerante e celosa. . . . Odiaba el término técnico, los vocablos eruditos, las palabras sesquipedales.' These tastes and qualities can be seen even in his short notices, like those which he wrote for the *Manchester Guardian*, a journal known for its exacting standards. But no work of this kind, however valuable, could be on a scale adequate to Fitzmaurice-Kelly's gifts. An interlude, of which he was always to speak as a happy one, and which gave him more leisure for concentration, was at hand.

I am not sure that in 1909 there were any Chairs of Spanish in Great Britain. One day Captain Gilmour, of the merchant service, who had spent some time in Latin America, entered the University of Liverpool and offered to found such a chair. The benefactor was welcomed, and the post, after our custom, was advertised to the world. It seemed that half the world had responded. The committee sat long sifting the candidates, some of whom sent their photographs, others their marriage certificates, others vouchers from municipal authorities. Three or four nations were represented. A number of the competitors were brilliant. Fitzmaurice-Kelly was appointed; he had not held a regular post before, but his record of work was irresistible. We did not know, nor did he, how he would like his new vocation. As it proved, he liked it greatly, and was himself greatly liked. Spanish was not taught in our secondary schools; and in a great commercial centre, on a new foundation, there could not be, at first, much chance of training scholars. What there was, the new professor seized; and he also punctually did the more rudimentary work demanded. For teaching purely mercantile Spanish there was other provision in the city. Fitzmaurice-Kelly could thus put his strength into reading and writing. He worked very hard, indeed too hard. The little house, called 'The Old Hall', an oasis in a suburb, which he shared with his friend Professor Wyld the philologist, was a cheerful resort for talk and company. With a friend or two, Fitzmaurice-Kelly conversed delightfully, with much wit, anecdote, and quotation; and he also listened well. But the house was also a laboratory. After the talk he would vanish and work late. His *annus mirabilis*, as a producer, was 1913. He now published his biography, *Miguel de Cervantes Saavedra*, in its definitive form; and *Littérature Espagnole*, 2e *édition*, *refondue et augmentée*, with its bibliography. This work he wrote in French himself. He also published *The Oxford Book of Spanish Verse*, xiii[th] *Century to xx[th] Century*, dedicated to his friend Don Santiago Pérez Triana. In this anthology, he liked especially to read aloud (and he was a very good reader) the verse of Rubén Darío. He was now fifty-six, in the fullness of his powers; and our University prides itself on having sheltered Fitz-

maurice-Kelly during these fruitful years. I have
no claim to speak, but am fortified by the opinion of
Sr. Sanín Cano in finding the preface to the *Oxford
Book* a beautiful and illuminating essay, in which the
author is freed from the enforced compression sometimes evident in his great *History*.

Fitzmaurice-Kelly also found time for other
activities that hitherto had been strange to him.
He took a notable part in academic affairs and
debates, which in our newer foundations are conducted on democratic lines. For a year he was
chairman of the Faculty of Arts; he also sat, spoke,
and made himself respected on the lay Council,
which is chiefly ruled by business men. He was
always with the progressive party, and threw himself into its cause with an unexpected warmth and
sharpness. His grave and courteous bearing covered
abundance of righteous scorn, and he was hard to
deceive. He left Liverpool in 1916 amid very
general regrets.

This was during the War. Fitzmaurice-Kelly
had gone to a recruiting-office, but was past the age
for acceptance. The War hit him hard. Two of
his house, a brother and a half-brother, were killed.
Though something of a cosmopolitan intellectually,
he was an ardent patriot; he had not come for
nothing of a soldier-stock. But he had to fall back
on his work; and he felt that he must accept the
offer of the new Cervantes Chair at King's College,
a leading institution of the London University.
Here, too, he would be near the great Reading-

Room of the Museum. He served four years at King's, still producing, and sometimes regretting Liverpool and his distance from his former circle. In 1920, being now sixty-three, he judged that it was time to retire from teaching. On this occasion he received a signal tribute from a band of fellow-scholars and friends. These included, besides colleagues from Liverpool, intimates of very long standing like Sir Edmund Gosse and Mr. R. B. Cunninghame-Grahame, and Spanish scholars such as Dr. Henry Thomas and Professor W. P. Ker. The address contained the following sentences, quoted afterwards in *The Times* obituary:

> Amid the national British awakening to the need of studies of the Spanish Motherland and of those
>
> ínclitas razas ubérrimas, sangre de España fecunda,
>
> now for a century in manifold union with ours, we take the occasion of your retirement from academic life to offer you from long intimacy a public tribute to the clear quality and intensity of your lifelong work, in accord with the high traditions of international culture among us, and to your pre-eminence as a scholar and critic.

Though hampered in his retreat by ill-health, Fitzmaurice-Kelly by no means stopped working. In 1918 he had married Miss Julia Sanders, daughter of the Rev. W. H. Sanders, herself a student of Spanish; and in this happy companionship he laboured on. He became editor, for Britain, of the *Hispanic Notes and Monographs*, published in Oxford; and amongst his many friends should be named Mr. Archer M. Huntington, president of the Hispanic Society. But I can make no effort to recount Fitzmaurice-Kelly's friends in Britain, France, Spain, and the two Americas. I do not know them, and any omissions must be pardoned. They are aware that he continued writing to the last. He published his *Primer of Spanish Literature* in 1922, and four posthumous works are in the press. The end came, after a brief last illness, on 30 November 1923.

Fitzmaurice-Kelly was a man of goodly presence and distinguished bearing, marked by a certain courteous aloofness to mere acquaintance. But under his armour, he was a man of close and deep affections, and a lover and favourite of children. Not tall, he had regular finely-moulded features and Irish eyes of a clear blue. He wore a beard and a cravat more after the Southern than the British fashion. His speech, like his gait, was deliberate; his voice agreeable, with a faintly non-English intonation, and his utterance fastidious. He was physically much more muscular than he looked, and was a good swimmer. He took a keen interest in cricket (which he played) and in some other sports. He travelled a good deal in Italy, Germany, and Scandinavia; and liked learning languages, which he was apt to do in the Underground Railway, through the medium of a Bible. His ideal of prose style has been indicated: an elegant ease and transparency, accompanied with a certain *finesse*. These qualities were very happily seen in his private letters. He cordially disliked public speaking, which, he felt, rather 'offended his *pudeur*'; and he never came to like it, though he came to do it well. His open lectures were at times too full of matter, but were relieved by a gentle irony, and were free from all tricks and gestures. His constitutional reticence, alluded to already, made it difficult for him to speak to many persons at once, even in print; and, in any case, he preferred to hide himself behind his work, and to speak through that.

# Notes

p. 9. *Style in Shakespeare.* Annual Shakespeare Lecture, read to the British Academy, 29 April 1936.

p. 9. *benefactors.* See list of the relevant works in Ebisch and Schücking's *S. Bibliography*, 1931, pp. 92–8. Besides the lexicons and glossaries (*O.E.D.*, Dyce, Schmidt, J. W. Cunliffe, and C. T. Onions), the grammars (Franz, Abbott), and Bartlett's *Complete Concordance*, the following will prove of special value for the study of Shakespeare's style: Henry Bradley, 'S.'s English', in *S.'s England*, 1916, ii. 539–74; Otto Jespersen, *Growth and Structure of the Eng. Language*, ed. 4, 1923, pp. 207–30, 'S. and the Language of Poetry'; George Gordon, *S.'s English*, tract no. xxix, for S.P.E., 1928. Also, for a more directly æsthetic treatment: George Ryland, 'S. the Poet', in *Companion to S. Studies*, 1934, pp. 89–115; J. W. Mackail, *The Approach to S.*, 1930, 1933, pp. 68, 133 ff.; Edmund Blunden, *S.'s Significances* (in *Lear*), 1929 (S. Association). Charles and Mary Cowden Clarke's *Shakespeare Key*, 1879, an old-fashioned miscellany, has many hints of value, anticipating later studies (of elliptical speech, iteration of phrases, slang and cant terms, dramatic uses of silence, etc.).

p. 10. *versification* (and prose). These are exhaustively discussed by Sir Edmund Chambers, *W.S.*, 2 vols., 1930, in their bearing on questions of revision, authenticity, date, etc.; but many of his comments bear directly on the poet's style and craft. See on the rapid alternations of verse and prose, and confusion between them, i. 182, 233, etc.; and on the evidences for date or order, as based on considerations of

263

style, i. 253 ff. (*'subject-matter has its reaction upon style'* (my italics) ). In deciding what is or is not an 'overflow', 'the elocutionary feeling must have the last word'. The 'verse-tests' (of which minute and often new statistics are given) are found to be chiefly of use, when determining authorship or sequence, as 'controls for the indications of external evidence' (i. 269 ff.).

p. 12. *A. C. Bradley.* As, for instance, in his paper on 'Monosyllabic Lines and Words in English Prose and Verse', in *A Miscellany*, 1929, pp. 245–67.

p. 12. *imagery.* See, too, the close and vivid study by Miss Elizabeth Holmes, *Aspects of Elizabethan Imagery*, 1929, pp. 37–71. Also G. Wilson Knight, *The Shakespearian Tempest*, 1932 (storm-imagery as a *leitmotiv* recurrent in the plays), and other works on similar lines.

p. 17. *critic of language.* Miss G. D. Willcock's paper, 1934, is issued by the S. Association. See, too, one by the same writer on 'S. and Elizabethan English', in *Companion*, pp. 117–36.

p. 21. *De Quincey.* On *Style* ; *Works*, ed. 1842, x. 171. For passage on p. 12 *ante*, see on *Shakespeare*, in *Works*, xv. 83.

p. 22. *euphuism.* The evidence is marshalled by E. Warwick Bond, *Works of John Lyly*, 1902, i. 164–75.

p. 30. *images kindle one another.* See, besides Miss Spurgeon's book, E. Kellett, *Suggestions*, 1923, pp. 57–78. 'On a Feature of S.'s Style', where this point is admirably made.

p. 33. *Matthew Arnold.* Many references, e.g. in his second lecture *On Translating Homer*, given in 1861.

p. 33. *George Saintsbury.* 'S. and the Grand Style', in *Essays and Studies of the Eng. Association*, 1910, vol. i, pp. 113–35.

p. 34. *Longinus on the Sublime*, ed. W. Rhys Roberts, 1899, ch. ix: ὕψος μεγαλοφροσύνης ἀπήχημα.

p. 37. *Spalding.* Published in 1833, the paper was

reprinted in N.S.S., series viii, no. 1, with *Life of Spalding* by J. Hill Burton (1876).

p. 38. *thorny grammar.* In *Coriolanus*, IV. vii. 35–53, speech of Aufidius: 'First he was A noble servant', etc.; and see the notes by Prof. R. H. Case in his 'Arden' edition of the play, 1922.

p. 42. *Electra of Sophocles.* I have used some words from Jebb's translation of ll. 1221, 1226.

p. 44. *The Present Value of Byron.* From the *Review of English Studies*, January 1925. The Byron Lecture, given at University College, Nottingham, 7 March 1924. Byron died on 19 April 1924. The lecture is here a good deal revised.

p. 70. *Robert Bridges and 'The Testament of Beauty.'* Presidential address to the English Association, 10 June 1922. The best comment is the *Notes* on this poem by Nowell C. Smith (O.U.P.).

p. 92. *Alexander Pushkin.* Read to the Royal Institution of Great Britain, 11 March 1938. The verse translations are my own, except where otherwise stated.

p. 118. *Chekhov.* The Taylorian Lecture, 1929, given in the Taylorian Institution, Oxford.

p. 135. This method is described at length by Mirsky, *Contemp. Russian Lit.*, 1926, p. 90, to whom I owe the hint.

p. 151. *Karel Čapek.* See Preface. The short article referred to appeared in *Life and Letters To-day*, June 1938.

p. 152. *Přítomnost.* See the numbers for 4 January 1939 and 29 December 1938.

p. 153. *translated.* By F. P. Marchant, Dora Round, F. P. Casey, and O. Vočadlo: *Painful Tales*, under the title *Money and other Stories.* Anonymously: *The Absolute Factory*, under the title *The Absolute at Large.* By Laurence Hyde: *Krakatit.* By Dora Round: *On Intimate Things.* By R. and M. Weatherall: *Nine Tales*, under the title *Fairy Tales*; *Dashenka*; *Hordubal*; *The Meteor*; *An Ordinary Life*; *The War with the Newts.* By Paul Selver: *Tales from One*

*Pocket* and *Tales from the Other Pocket,* in one volume (with some omissions), under the title *Tales from Two Pockets.* A translation of *The First Rescue Party* is announced (May 1938) as in preparation. I have not come on any English version of *Shining Deeps* or of *Calvaries.*

p. 163. *noetic.* The word in Czech, Dr. Wellek informs me, is equivalent to ' epistemological'—what concerns the theory of knowledge; it is here contrasted with 'ethical', as the passage shows.

p. 191. *Reason and Enthusiasm in the Eighteenth Century.* The Adamson Memorial Lecture, given in the University of Manchester, 31 May 1923. In *Essays and Studies by Members of the English Association,* vol. x, 1924.

p. 206. He goes yet further in a phrase quoted in *N.E.D.*: 'It is the believing those to be miracles which are not, that constitutes an enthusiast' (*Princ. of Methodism,* p. 54, 1746).

p. 207. The *Letter concerning Enthusiasm* (1708), *The Moralists, a Rhapsody* (1709), and the *Miscell. Reflections* (1711), together furnish the material. I keep the old printing, which is part of the author's manner, from my edition (the 'second, corrected', 1714).

p. 213. *The Nature of Literary Criticism.* Lecture on the Ludwig Mond Foundation, given in the University of Manchester, 11 January 1935.

p. 214. L. Abercrombie, *Principles,* etc., 1933; first published in *An Outline of Modern Knowledge,* 1931, pp. 860–907. See especially the discussion of the *Poetics* and of Horace.

p. 215. Lamb, *Specimens of English Dramatic Poets,* etc. (1808), on *The White Devil* (Cornelia's song).

p. 217. Croce: *Æsthetic,* tr. D. Ainslie, ed. 2, 1922; *Essence of Æsthetic,* tr. Ainslie, 1921; *Defence of Poetry,* tr. E. F. Carritt, 1934 (Oxford lecture). See too ch. ix ('Theory of Beauty') in H. Wildon Carr, *Philosophy of Benedetto Croce,* 1917. The most pertinent chapter for the present purpose is in *Essence*, etc., pp. 83–104 (*La critica letteraria come filosofia*, in *Nuovi Saggi di Estetica*, ed. 1926, pp. 203–15.)

p. 218.   I. A. Richards, *Principles of Literary Criticism*, 1925; *Practical Criticism*, 1929.

p. 219.   *Defence of Poetry*, pp. 26–7.

p. 220.   J. Sampson, *In Lighter Moments*, 1934, p. 82.

p. 222.   Croce on the hedonist; *Defence of Poetry*, p. 24 (poetry regarded as a 'secretion', etc.).   On impressionism generally (e.g. as in Jules Lemaître), see *La Critica letteraria* (*q.v.* also for his judgement on Sainte-Beuve, for starting not with *estetica* as he should but with 'lo studio morale'—in Croce's view a topsy-turvy procedure).   Some shrewd cuts at A. E. Housman and his lecture can be found in J. Bronowski, *The Poet's Defence*, C.U.P., 1939, pp. 209 ff.

p. 223.   Montague, *A Writer's Notes*, 1930, p. 3.

p. 225.   Longinus, *De Sublimitate*, ch. xxxv, ed. and tr. W. Rhys Roberts, 1899, p. 135.   For a valuable survey, see T. R. Henn, *Longinus and English Criticism*, Cambridge, 1934.

p. 228.   'each single work of art.'   For a compact statement, see *Breviario*, p. 47: 'il senso artistico e poetico, il quale ama ciascun' opera in sé, per quello che essa è, come una creatura viva, individua e incomparabile, e sa che ogni opera ha la sua individua legge e il suo pieno e insostituibile valore.'   For Croce's view of further 'value', see *La Critica Letteraria, ad fin.*: 'true and complete criticism is the serene historical narration of what has happened':—a finding that appears either to shelve the question, or to end in sheer relativity.

p. 231.   *Timon of Athens*, IV. iii. 26 ff.

p. 232.   Dante, *De Vulgari Eloquio*, ii. 4: 'stilo equidem tragico tunc uti videmur, quando cum gravitate sententiæ tam superbia carminum, quam constructionis elatio, et excellentia vocabulorum concordat.'

See *Latin Works of Dante* (Temple Classics), p. 79.

## Notes

p. 236. Johnson on *Paradise Lost; Lives of the Poets* (Milton), ed. G. Birkbeck Hill, 1905, i. 183.

p. 237. *Causeries du Lundi*, 24 October 1850; ed. 1852, iii. 31–44, 'Qu'est-ce qu'un classique?'

p. 239. *George Saintsbury.* From *Life and Letters*, June 1933. A memoir of Saintsbury for the British Academy (1933), by the present writer, was published by the Oxford University Press and is also in the *Proceedings* of the Academy. There is a much fuller one by Professor A. Blyth Webster in the *University of Edinburgh Journal*, autumn number, 1933, pp. 30–72.

p. 250. *James Fitzmaurice-Kelly.* From *Revue Hispanique*, tome lx, 1924. It is there followed by an appreciation by Mr. Aubrey F. G. Bell; and by a bibliography of F.-K.'s Hispanic studies, the work of Mrs. Fitzmaurice-Kelly. The article upon him in the *D.N.B.*, 1922–30, is by Prof. W. J. Entwistle.

pp. 251, 255. *Menéndez y Pelayo, Prólogo*, pp. xx–xxi, to F.-K.'s *Hist. de la Literatura española*, Madrid, 1901.

# Index

# Index

# Index

271

# Index

273

# Index

274

# Index